Orange Alert

Kazim Ali

Orange Alert

ESSAYS ON POETRY, ART,
AND THE ARCHITECTURE
OF SILENCE

THE UNIVERSITY OF MICHIGAN PRESS
Ann Arbor

2013   2012   2011   2010   4   3   2   1

A CIP catalog record for this book is available from the British Library.

Library of Congress Cataloging-in-Publication Data

Ali, Kazim, 1971–
    Orange alert : essays on poetry, art and the architecture of
silence / Kazim Ali.
        p. cm. — (Poets on Poetry)
    ISBN 978-0-472-07127-2 (cloth : alk. paper) — ISBN 978-0-472-
05127-4 (pbk. : alk. paper)
    1. Poetics.   2. Silence in literature.   I. Title.
PS3601.L375O73   2010
809.1'9353—dc22   2010014034

to Layla Al-Attar

The Sacral Chakra is symbolized by a lotus with six petals, and corresponds to the colour orange . . . Mentally it governs creativity, emotionally it governs joy, and spiritually it governs enthusiasm.

—Patricia Mercier, *The Chakra Bible*

The current threat advisory level has been raised to orange.
—U.S. Department of Homeland Security,
2001 and onward

Acknowledgments

Grateful acknowledgment to the editors of the following publications where these essays, in earlier versions, first appeared: *American Poetry Review:* "From the Open Sea," "Ersatz Everything," "The Architecture of Loneliness," "Faith and Silence," "Write Something on My Wall"; *AWP Writers Chronicle:* "Guardian of the Gates of Paradise: Form and Disunity in Agha Shahid Ali"; *Barn Owl Review:* "adam and his mother: Lucille Clifton's Prosody"; *Center:* a portion of "On the Line"; *Inside Higher Ed:* "Poetry Is Dangerous"; *Kenyon Review:* "In the Hurricane's Eye"; *Kenyon Review On-Line:* a portion of "On the Line"; *The Millions:* "Why We Need Poetry Now"; *Kenyon Review On-Line:* "Little Map: A Valentine"; *National Book Critics Circle Small Press Spotlight:* "A Brief Poetics: To Layla Al-Attar"; *Poetry Foundation:* "Poetry and Dance," "Poetry and Music," "Poetry and Painting," "Poetry and Community," "Poetry and Silence," "illuminate I could"; *Xcp (Cross-Cultural Poetics):* an earlier version of "How to Speak" (as "Twelve Questions").

"Radha Says" was published as the introduction to *Radha Says,* by Reetika Vazirani (Drunken Boat Media, 2010).

"The Future Tense of History" was drawn from "Yoko Ono: Art, Consumption, and Survival," a talk given at The Poetry Project at St. Mark's Church in January 2004. A preliminary version was delivered at the Central New York Conference on Language and Literature at SUNY Cortland in October 2003.

Thank you to Hyder Aga, Anselm Berrigan, Edan Lepucki, Leslie McGrath, Mark Nowak, Shona Ramaya, Robin Schaer, Jason Schneiderman, Ravi Shankar, Prageeta Sharma, Jane Sprague, Nick Twemlow, and Emily Warn for supporting this work in obvious and unobvious ways.

For years of steadfast support and kindness, my thanks to Jennifer Chapis, Tim Doyle, Stephen Motika, April Ossmann, Sean Safford, Marco Wilkinson, and Marion Wrenn.

Thank you to Michael Bibby, Todd Crawley, Catherine Dent, Carla Kungl, Sharra McCallum, Susan Osberg, Tiffany Saylor, Kim van Alkemade, and Rich and Ami Zumkhawala-Cook. To Annie Finch, Marilyn Hacker, Ellen Bauerle, Alexa Ducsay, and all at the University of Michigan Press.

To Helen Elam and Judith Johnson.

Thank you to Oberlin College for a Powers Travel Grant, which aided in the writing of "The Architecture of Loneliness," and to my many supportive colleagues there. Thank you to Ammiel Alcalay and Fady Joudah for answering many clarifying questions.

Thank you to Paula McLain and Philip Metres for invaluable editorial advice.

And great and special thanks to Elizabeth Scanlon, editor extraordinaire, who invited me to write a series of essays for the *American Poetry Review*.

And I owe a great debt to my research assistant Max Rivlin-Nadler, for his priceless assistance in tracking down sources, preparing endnotes and generally keeping me on track in the home stretch.

Contents

1.

Poetry and Dance   1

From the Open Sea: Body and Lyric in the Poetry of
  Jane Cooper   5

The Guardian of the Gates of Paradise   25

In the Hurricane's Eye: On Mahmoud Darwish   34

Poetry and Music   43

Yoko Ono's "Mulberry": The Future Tense of History   49

How to Speak   52

2.

Poetry and Painting   63

Radha Says: Considering the Last Poems of
  Reetika Vazirani   68

Little Map: A Valentine   73

Poetry and Community   82

Poetry Is Dangerous   90

The Architecture of Loneliness   93

A Brief Poetics: To Layla Al-Attar   120

3.

Poetry and Silence   123

adam and his mother: Lucille Clifton's Prosodic Line   128 illuminate she could: Lucille Clifton's Lucifer   137

On the Line; or, The Poetics of Twitter   143

Ersatz Everything: The Value of Meaning   147

Write Something on My Wall: Body, Identity and Poetry   170

Why We Need Poetry Now   187

Faith and Silence   190

1

Poetry and Dance

One cool Saturday evening, early spring, I sat on the train platform of the Marble Hill station, looking out at the Hudson
River, Inwood Forest beyond it, the sun setting behind the
rocks. A couple of years earlier, on the eve of the war, some of
the sangha members from the Village Zendo buried an Earth
Treasure, a clay pot filled with bone fragments and ashes of a
deceased rinpoche, somewhere in the forest as part of a prayer
for peace.

It reminds me of Maya Lin's Peace Chapel installation at
Juniata College in Central Pennsylvania. Lin's chapel has two
elements—the public chapel, a circular gathering place made
of big uncarved granite blocks, and then a private reflection
point, on the ridge above the chapel, a small metal disk set into
the forest floor.

There is a secret place buried deep in the forest, the hillside,
the body. The secret place is the prayer for peace.

Cool wind, spring evening—it was a version of heaven there,
on the train platform. I had just come from a daylong meeting,
much debate, a lot of emotion. I was feeling tense, distracted,
wrung out. What I suddenly wanted to do was unclench, and
stretch myself open. I've done yoga in public places before—in
transit lounges, in parks, in hotel conference rooms—but that
evening on the concrete, in the darkening, it seemed perhaps
the river was enough yoga.

The next day, the river still on my mind, I went to work with
the choreographer Susan Osberg, who was putting together an

evening of work called "Dancing on Water." Her show was to include modern dancers, ballet dancers and a step troupe. I would be reading poems and performing two solo dances. It had been nearly two years since I danced on stage, but I was really excited to be working with Susan, whose approach to dance is very intuitive, and rooted in emotional response; she is a poet and poetry lover besides.

We started by turning on some Sufi trance music and just moving in space, trying to feel the essence of liquid or water, since my poems both deal with rain. Susan had me read one poem several times, and we settled on three words from the poem to work with. She broke the words down into a movement vocabulary, and we improvised the phrases. Soon, slowly, the amorphous movements began to coalesce, and Susan moved to one side, observing my body's movements and directing me.

The process is not unlike that of writing a poem, with a key difference. In dance there is always an audience. Perhaps sometimes only the choreographer or teacher, or even more radically, perhaps only a mirror. But does a dance really depend on "being seen"? In Yoko Ono's *Bag Piece,* the performers climb inside a huge black bag, seal it up and perform inside. The viewer experiences the motions of the body only visually, and from a remove. In her *Touch Piece,* the lights are turned out, and one experiences the performance by touch only.

I dream of poems that dream of such dance.

In the writing process there is always a secret that is being kept, a disk embedded in the forest floor from which one observes the phenomenal world.

Rumi, one of my spirit guides, created his works in dialogue with a community. My other spirit guide, Lalla, wandered naked in the wilderness. It is possible that the one is not opposite of the other.

Susan structured a dance from my poem "Rain," and had me rehearse it over and over while she gave me directions, ideas for tightening the physical phrase, demonstrating the moves to me. It turned out that after feeling the poem in my body in such a way, it moved in the world through me completely differently. This is not a poem I often perform at readings, yet I understood the architecture of it now in a purely physical way. In the second poem we worked from whole phrases rather than words, but rather than increase in complexity, the dance stilled even more into slower movements, held positions.

"There is a wind that never dies," writes Yoko Ono, and there is energy that moves through art in its creation that the art approximates but is mere record of.[1] To bury a pot in the forest is a long hope for peace—an understanding of erosion and the slow moving of water through the biosphere. This is the physical part of dance that poetry dreams about.

There are other parts of body-practice, of course, that can inform poetry in purely actual ways. My yoga practice taught me an evening and restraint of breath that has helped me understand the rhythm of a line. Understanding the syntax of the body has helped me appreciate and adore poetry of great heart that uses a joyful undoing of syntax. Thinking about the choreography of the body in space has taught me a real appreciation for physical spaces and silences in the page itself. And my favorite form of dancing, *butoh*, with its restraints and stillness, has taught me a love for the pared down, the evocative and provocative barely there.

And the body is alive—warm and muscular and kinetic, but also tender, loving and vulnerable. When I write poems I am always either writing backwards—in my case, to Rumi, to Lalla, to Emily Dickinson, to Agha Shahid Ali—or perhaps forwards to the unknown and terrible. It is hard to write to this minute. But the body is a lovely, temporary temple—subject to aging, promised to die. Dance cannot help but be tied to this direct moment, to this day only.

At the end of the dance I was doing for Susan, I would approach a book on the stage and read from it one of my own poems. The poem is about the Hudson River and its curious phenomenon: though the river flows from its source out to the sea, the ocean water rushes back up. There is a place where the ocean water eddies, and returns.

I only want to actually be in this world and write to this world. Death was promised to me at my birth. I am saying back to it my peaceful life.

In every dance there should be a secret place where promises are made.

NOTE

1. Yoko Ono, "To The Wesleyan People," in *YES Yoko Ono,* ed. John Hendricks and Alexandra Munroe (New York: Harry N. Abrams, 2000), 288.

From the Open Sea

Body and Lyric in the Poetry of Jane Cooper

I met Jane Cooper once in my life, white light of the afternoon pouring through the windows of her Upper West Side apartment. It was late afternoon, spring of 2001, and the sound of the earth moving beneath us seemed at last obvious. Jane moved very deliberately, making our tea, performing each activity: opening the cupboard, taking out cups, pouring water into the kettle. Not one thing was a hinge moment, a transition from one thing to another; at no moment was Jane performing two tasks at once; each moment belonged to itself.

Which is to say, when she looked at me, she looked at me. When she spoke to me, she spoke to me. The space between two figures in the painting in her hallway, the space between the word she spoke and when I heard it and then the next word. Her body existed in that room, in that space, at the beginning of another era in our history, but that moment when it still seemed we might move toward peace, might move away from what now seems an inevitably impending endless war.

In her prose poem "The Past," Jane writes of being treated as a child by a doctor whose uncle fought in the war of 1812. The poem concludes, "And how do I connect in my own body—that is, through touch—the War of 1812 with the smart rocket nosing its way via CNN down a Baghdad street? How much can two arms hold? How soon will my body, which already spans a couple of centuries, become almost transparent and begin to shiver apart?"[1]

Cooper held the mortal moment—the moment of the body's failure—as close as she held the breath in the heart of her poems. In between her poems' lines was that pause of silence between one thing and another, a moment that acknowledged bodies' separation from one another, the compassion they owed one another as mortal objects. This mere recognition of compassion seems so important in the present moment, a compassion that requires a principled opposition to all violence and war, a commitment to work toward other solutions.

By the end of her life, of course, Cooper's body would—like all of ours eventually—shiver apart, like a treasure of the earth, dispersing its passions to those connected to her only briefly—including me, a lonely schoolteacher who knew very few poets at all, writing to her out of the blue, in need of hearing any news at all of the earth's survival, anything at all. If in a hundred years future generations want to know what it *felt* like to be alive and human through war, bomb tests, genetic engineering of the food supply and the dehumanization inherent in the spread of global capital and its attendant de-democratized national and supernational political institutions, one can only pray that among the poems in the time capsule are hers.

It's a panic, I admit—that the individual's body doesn't mean anything in the face of the machinations of the state and the corporation. That to *be* an individual at all, with one's own perceptions, hopes and compassions, is political in the extreme. To refuse cruelty—to refuse to participate in the machine of production and consumption that global capital both enables and requires for survival—is practically unpatriotic. One has to talk about politics when talking about Jane Cooper because her concerns are human—individual and human—and so wedded as a conscientious refusal of what might otherwise seem the inevitable advance of "civilization," which is anything but "civil."

In an early poem called "Letters" Cooper presents an idea of the individual body fluidly woven into the fabric of time, the surrounding world, the processes of aging and decay inherent in life. In the first section of the poem she writes:

> That quiet point of light
> trembled and went out.
>
> Iron touches a log:
> it crumbles to coal, then ashes.

> The log sleeps in its shape.
> A new moon rises.
>
> Darling, my white body
> still bears your imprint.[2]

When the log succumbs to its natural process—not burned here but rather "touched" by the iron—it does not disappear but "sleeps in its shape." The new moon rising is an image of presence-by-absence—a moon real and extant but completely invisible. The speaker herself at last appears as the body that appears in the final couplet—a body that is also the log, the ash that remains, also the moon in the sky, also the quiet point of light of the first line. These are all things in the world that disappear and even after their disappearance have a life by what remains of them.

The second half of the poem shifts both sonically and physically, from outside to inside:

> Wind chewed at the screen,
> rain clawed at the window.
>
> Outside three crows
> make their harsh, rainy scraping.
>
> Autumn has come
> in early July.
>
> On the ground white petals:
> my rain-soaked letters.

We're immediately, in the second section, in the world of humans: inside a house protected from the howling elements that both "chew" and "claw," the wind, the rain, the crows. It's an unseasonable climactic shift in this short poem about mortality and endings, bodies becoming not what they were, autumn arriving two months early. The "letters" on the ground are gorgeous—"white petals" and "rain-soaked" but also heavy with meaning—they are communiqués from the speaker, things dropped on the ground, what remain after life, but also letters as in elemental parts of the communication itself. A body does not disappear but unravels itself, sheds its meanings into the earth.

When I see her spare couplets I remember her moving around the kitchen slowly, deliberately, warming the cups with hot water, placing objects on a tray: the cups, a sugar dish, a creamer. The body determines how one experiences the actual world and so also impacts the shape of poetic form and how it tries to transmit experience. Cooper's poetic lines build themselves across the page in couplets, first one line then the other—you have to hear the line and the space around it.

Cooper writes here a poem about death and the changing of the seasons and ends it with letters dropped on the ground, the tree's white petals—images of beauty and transmission, in short what you would normally think of as life itself. It would be a mistake though to think of her vision of death as purely optimistic or needlessly sentimental. In her early poem "The Weather of Six Mornings" she comments on the possibilities of communication and transference with a little bit of a starker tone:

> Sunlight lies along my table
> like abandoned pages.
>
> I try to speak
> of what is so hard for me
>
> —this clutter of a life—
> Puritanical signature![3]

But in each of the six short lyrics that make up the poem cycle, Cooper does not try for a "resolution" at all; rather, each poem, loosely arranged, arrives at a failing point—a place where the poet stops pushing against the ineffable. In this way, the poems—not an "epic" at all, but a form of "serial lyric"—accumulate into a quieter, more resigned wisdom than "epiphany." The little creatures of the natural world here, "insects, / pine needles, birch leaves // make a ground bass of silence / that never quite dies."

As these leaves, creatures, needles on the ground—as the letters from the previous poem—create a silence, the speaker hovers in the face of it, wondering what is the appropriate response. Moments of anticipation govern the couplets of the following section:

Treetops are shuddering
in uneasy clusters

like rocking water
whirlpooled before a storm.

Words knock at my breast,
heave and struggle to get out.

A black-capped bird
pecks on, unafraid.

Yield then, yield
to the invading rustle of the rain!

Her fear of expressing herself is contrasted with the unafraid bird, but it is not purely oppositional—even the trees in the earlier couplet are shown to shudder. It's interesting that the action of yielding to the rain, an acceptance of the world's actions as superior and more important than the human struggle to communicate, finishes the piece. It is not really a sublimation of the self to nature but rather a release of the individual ego into the fact of larger existence. Against the Platonic ideal of man as measure of the universe, Cooper situates herself not as an individual body/spirit responding to a Creator, but rather as a constituent part of Creation.

Though Cooper yields to the rain here, in the following poem she finds that "a man's voice / refuses to be absorbed." The distance of her friend's death is incomprehensible, and though the friend's ashes "float out to sea," Cooper still hungers for "some marker." We want to know that the human body, the individual person, will still be remembered, still matters in some way. The burning of a body to ashes and subsequent dispersal of those ashes is the deepest form of metaphor for the soul's ultimate anxiety: that it is mortal, that death is eternal, that the self is annihilated upon its separation from carnate matter.

This anxiety plays out in seven lines of conditional clause in a mere ten-line poem. "If the weather breaks / I can speak of your dying," Cooper reasons, but after five more lines she says also, "I can speak of your living," grammatically equating the two actions as the same action.

Once again Cooper does not come across as an optimist. It's

the disappearing friend, the parting of the two that preoccupies her:

> Now all the years in between
> flutter away like lost poems
>
> And the morning light is so delicate,
> so utterly empty . . .
>
> at high altitude, after long illness,
> breathing in mote by mote a vanished world . . .

The dissolution of the physical association of the two made by the friend's departure, the dispersal of the years into wind and light, the empty light, the subtlety and quietness with which these images are drawn all serve to create a tender emotional mood in the final line—"mote by mote a vanished world"—with the final ellipsis drifting into silence.

Again the white light is filtering through the curtain windows, Jane is putting her cup down into her saucer with the lightest clinking. I'm sitting back in the cushions, feeling unkempt, clumsy, too loud whenever I try to answer one of her questions. I sent Jane a few poems after that, and she wrote back to me several times. We tried a few times to meet again before she left New York City but didn't manage it. I would often guiltily swipe up any used copies of *The Flashboat* I could find— guiltily because I was denying other poetry lovers the chance to find this book, but it is the one book I continued to give as gifts to anyone I needed to. I would have a stash of them on my bookshelf just to give away. When I couldn't explain poetry or why I write it to myself or anyone else, I had this book.

When I was working on final versions of my own poems for the publication of my first book, *The Far Mosque,* I always held the last poem of the sequence, "The Weather of Six Mornings," in my head. To be specific, it was the final three lines of the poem:

> Rest.
> A violin bow, a breeze
>
> just touches the birches.
> Cheep—a new flute

tunes up in a birch top.
A chipmunk's warning skirrs . . .

Whose foot disturbs these twigs?
To the sea of received silence

why should I sign
my name?

What's resting can be the poem itself, all creation or that violin
bow. A bow at rest on a string is preparing to make music or has
just completed it—either way the music's silence resonates like
the breeze, the baby bird in the tree, the chipmunk. After all the
animal speech—a noisy poem after all—the presence of a human
foot on twigs seems unbearable and unnecessary, leading to the
stunning final question. What reason, then, Cooper asks, to add
anything at all to the silent sound of creation?

But that stunning question of Cooper's—made more magnificent by its publication as the closing poem of her first collection—is meant to be not rhetorical but real. She does not
leave it hanging in space, but spends a career at the liminal edge
of silence, negotiating the relationship between an individual
and corporeal existence and the fact of creation. The poetry
may seem spiritual, but it is precisely the border between the
tangible body and the ineffable nature of the spirit that Cooper
seeks to know and understand.

Like many writers who came of age during World War II and
its aftermath, Jane Cooper first wrote work that engaged humans in a landscape of war. She comments on the relationship
between beauty and experience: "I never could get over the
peculiar beauty of a bombed out landscape," she writes of her
experiences in Europe after the war, though conceding she only
saw this landscape "once the worst had been cleaned up, once
the summer field flowers—poppies and fireweed and ragwort—
had seeded themselves and started blooming over the rubble."
She could not help but feel "guilt because I found the desolation visually beautiful."

Additionally, after writing an entire book of these poems—
which would have been her first collection, a book she referred
to as a "woman's experience of war"—she stopped writing and

never tried to publish them. She engages the question of why she stopped writing in her long essay "Nothing Has Been Used in the Manufacture of This Poetry That Could Have Been Used in the Manufacture of Bread," which she reprinted in each of the two books following her debut collection. She initially claims, as Grace Paley suggested, that "men's lives seemed more central than ours, almost more truthful."[4] It's true that Cooper most frequently positions herself in these political poems as a witness, an observer, someone who exists in the war only peripherally, not implicated. Only much later, in poems like "Clementene" and "Hotel de Dream," does Cooper explicitly confront her own complicity in oppression and the war, which a position as bystander or witness to atrocity encompasses. In Cooper's case it is her "sensuous, precious, upper-class / unjust white child's past" that she must come to terms with. In "Clementene" Cooper writes of her shock as a young girl when she learns that one of the tailors who worked for her family had been passing for white. "Why, if I was not an accomplice," Cooper wonders, "did I feel— do I feel still—this complex shame?"[5]

Despite feelings of guilt from necessary implication in the forces of history—even these days every one of us is contributing nearly fifty-five cents from every single one of our tax dollars to the U.S. military budget, the highest percentage of the overall national budget of any nation in the world—Cooper, in the remarkable poem "The Flashboat," which takes place as a dream, describes the challenges of stepping out of the role of "witness" and into the role of actual participant.

In the dream, a ship is sinking, a bell is ringing, the ice around the ship is breaking apart. In this dire situation, one of the ship's officers—"my torturer who assumes we think alike"— is interrogating Cooper. "Are you a political activist?" he asks. To which she replies, "No, I'm a teacher." It's the wrong answer— he confiscates her passport and locks it away. "Was I wrong to declare myself innocent?" she wonders.

At the end of the poem, the ship is sinking, the crew are making ready the lifeboats and she is offered either a space on a larger, comfortable boat with the other women and the captain in charge, or a position on the smaller "flashboat," which will require everyone to row, to lead the way to rescue. She writes, "For a moment, I hesitate, worrying about my defective blood," but then:

> My voice with its crunch of bone wakes me: *I choose the flashboat!*
>   work,
>   the starry waters[6]

That mention of a voice with a "crunch of bone" is wonderful and ominous, and it also signals the breaking of the poem from prose paragraphs to three verse lines at the end, the final two indented for added emphasis. Of particular subtle effect is the comma following the word "work" which changes its meaning from a verb into a more powerful and ongoing presence as a noun. The idea of "work," the rowing of the flashboat, is also equated with the starry waters themselves, making action of any kind not a transitive condition leading from a beginning to a desired result, but rather a fixed quality of motion in the world, an eternity of breath, a body that exists, a universe that depends on inflow and outflow, perpetual "action."

She does therefore "implicate" herself as a positive agent, whether she was a "bystander" or not during the war years.

In "Nothing Has Been Used in the Manufacture of This Poetry," she goes on to reveal the true reason she could not publish the earlier poems: she "couldn't face out the full range of intuition" the poems revealed. Even in her writing about war and bodies in a general sense, she was facing the more frightening subject of liminality between the life of the body and its death, the sounds of the world at peace and war, and their cessation. There is, after all, something truly horrifying about the silence at the end of bombing, the silence at the end of a storm, at the end of the bomb tests. "Why did I feel the need," she asks herself, "to write about the holocaust almost more than individual human relations, or to disguise my purpose to myself?" She goes on to realize, "In any case, by 1951 the war had begun to seem like a mask, something to write *through* in order to express a desolation that had become personal."

So when Cooper poses the question in 1969—"To the sea of received silence // why should I sign / my name?"—she asks of herself a real question past this question, not just with a spiritual dimension referring to the problem of the human body within the matrix of creation, but another question with real material and political consequences: how can one write about the body as it exists in the world, remaining true to the individual life but conscious of the problematic dehumanization the twentieth century seemed to be engendering? Her answer to both of these questions simultaneously was a stunning series of poems written in the last two decades of her writing life, many of which, like her earlier poems, she withheld from publication until the 2000 release of *The Flashboat: Poems Collected and Reclaimed.*

Did the poems feel too personal, too hermetic? Did she see them as primarily building blocks representing hinge moments in her poetics from period to period? At any rate, they are charged with energy and space, dynamic and alarming; they now feel like essential documents anticipating in many ways the space-laden, fractured yet intensely personal lyrics of many younger poets writing today.

Cooper wrote her way out of her earlier, more formal work. Large spaces began opening up in the poems, not only literal silences but silences of energy, much the way large flat color panes rise out of and interrupt the otherwise frenetic energy of Hoffmann's canvases. Her poem "Messages" answers back—in style at least—to the delicate couplets of "The Weather of Six Mornings" or "Letters":

> Ragged and thrashing
> the road between me and the ocean—
>
> I trip on stumps.
> A gull flies over:
>
> Guilt! guilt! your father is dying!
> The woods are studded with poisonous berries.[7]

The energy is very different here from the quiet and deliberate lines of the earlier poems. Lines are interrupted, and the couplets themselves are split in action between the first line and the second line. As the speaker trips, the bird flies over but does not speak until the first line of the next couplet. But the second line of that couplet does not complete the thought, but rather moves on into the landscape. Besides the quick shifts in energy, the tripping of both sound and speaker, the poem introduces an idea of opposition, things that can be one thing or another:

> a few stars telegraph:
> Go back. Or else welcome.

These "Messages" are very different from the communiqués of "Letters," where the speaker felt herself dissolving into creation, participating in it, dropping her letters down as leaves or petals fall, part of a natural dissolution. The speaker here is troubled, resistant, unsure how it is one is able to send her message— rather than writing delicate and rhapsodic couplets, a seamless communication, the later poet is anxious, frustrated, and finally communicates the only way she dares—in bits and pieces, not like a letter at all, but closer to the telegraph communication of the stars:

> Approaching my life I am terrified.
> Stars in the mud trip me up.
>
> Terrified, I lug stone after stone
> up the wide, foot-bruising ladder of night.
>
> Stones in a ring can't define it:
> Night. Lake. Mirror.   Deep.   Only

Needless to say—or perhaps one needs indeed to say it—the last line is a stunner, not only in the context of Cooper's work but in the context of the poem itself. It is the breakdown of the sentence and possibility of meaning, but simultaneously a wholesale trust in language itself to make meaning. We travel into the atmosphere of the lake, word by word, deeper and deeper until the final word—a word of singularity, a word of doubt, ultimately a word of conclusion, but thank god for Jane Cooper's trust in the absolute energy of silence to forgo the final period, which if added would have undone the whole motion of the poem. She is that much a master of subtlety that a single punctuation mark re-moved—or added where it does not belong as we saw in the final moment of "The Flashboat"—can sound volumes of resonance. She tries here in "Messages" to begin documenting her work at allowing the "received silence"—the silence of poetry, the silence after war, the silence of awe in the soul—into her body, her days, her noiseful life.

"Scattered Words for Emily Dickinson" and "S. Eliason 66"—both poems written in the 1970s but withheld from publication until 2000—are companion poems of sorts, each about the painting hanging in Cooper's apartment; The painting was done by Cooper's friend Shirley Eliason and depicts Dickinson and her friend Charles Wadsworth, one of the men speculated to be the recipient of her infamous "Master Letters."

"Scattered Words" unfolds in three short sections of lyric writing, narrative description, a list of "scattered words" and a piece of found text. It imitates (and prefigures in the next poem) Dickinson's desperate and powerful attachment to Wadsworth, one which like all of Dickinson's attachments remained somehow necessarily *detached* in the final account. The body of the poem squirms away from its subject, and the energy raised up has nowhere else to go but the next poem. At first glance a reader would say a poem like this is a failure or maybe at most the first half of a poem which has no second half, but perhaps more honestly it was thirty years ahead of its time—Cooper had to wait a little while for the light inside the text to be seen for what it was: a visionary explanation of the subject/body's tenuous relationship to the lyric. A poem that escapes poetry. Meaning it is still breathing on the page.

The poem's short first section reads:

> Inside the crate, dark
> as corn in its sheath   sheet lightning[8]

The enjambment between lines and the lacuna in the second line, the wordplay across that space—"sheath   sheet"—create an intimate and energetic space. One thinks the painting in its crate, radiating energy, is something of a stand-in for the figures themselves depicted there, their passion barely contained.

    at the conservatory door   they

    start forth

    flashbulbs!

    ochre orange flame black black white

Their energy is purely transformed by the flashbulb of the painter's attention, scholars going through Dickinson's private letters and speculating about her most intimate relationships like paparazzi of the present moving backwards in time. The moment of the flashbulbs is a hinge between the dynamism of the couple—again unfolding with unusual enjambment and lacuna—and the "scattered words" themselves. The energy here is not allowed to explode out, but rather, from the chaotic chain of words, Cooper introduces found text from the exhibit catalogue:

> *Brilliant Pioneer Roots* and
> *difficult geography of the face of a friend:*
> (brilliant) notes from the painter's (my friend's) catalogue
> (difficult) notes from the painter's (a pioneer's) catalogue

With the lovely parentheticals Cooper allows the "brilliance" and "difficulty" to be both acknowledged and unsaid, to be "background" in the painting sense. She also imposes her personal connection to the work in the second parenthetical—in the first line linking herself with Eliason, in the second line crucially linking Eliason to Dickinson herself. She puts herself in the poem personally, the way Eliason finds herself inside Dickinson. This occupation of one body inside the other is exactly what was happening in the earlier poem "Messages"—the body of the poem inside the poem.

Oppositional philosophies of the body and spirit are either dualistic—saying the body is the mortal part and the spirit is immortal—or nondualistic—saying the body and the spirit are inherently wedded, one in the same being. Cooper, on the other hand, wrestles with the separation of writer of the poem and poem, painter and subject painted. These musings take us back to the initial lines of the first section, which have no immediate referent until the mention of the painting in the second numbered section. One is reminded of the poet herself inside the crate of her poem, also of Dickinson, declining to sign her first letter to Higginson, instead signing a small card which she sealed in a second smaller envelope to include with the unsigned letter. A body inside a body inside a body.

Then fabulously, what does the poem do with this fever of images, this back-and-forth set of readings in the first two sections? It moves into a completely unrelated scene in the third section:

> So the stolid-looking veteran
> (G.I. Bill, History of the Language)
> told me, speaking of combat:
>> *In the least space*
>> *between two bodies*
>> *there is room*
>> *for mystery*

She takes us completely away from the painting itself to another figure having a conversation with her about a different subject, so we are meant to travel some distance by applying his speech metaphorically to the painting we have heard described. His speech is not reported in a prose line but in poetic lines that freight the breaks with space and distance: "space," "bodies," "room" and "mystery" allowing the starkness of the painting, the moment it depicts, to fill us at the end of the poem.

It's the least space between two bodies that resonates the most—between Dickinson and Wadsworth, between the painting and its case, between Eliason and her work, between Cooper and the poem. It's a mystery, the last line of the poem tells us, it is "sheet lightning," the opening section says, but most of all we end up remembering the veteran himself is not talking about painting or poetry, but about combat and death.

Is it enough to delineate the tense moment between creator and creation, to point out that art cannot contain its subject at all or be contained by it, that even—as we know—Dickinson cannot yet approach Dickinson? Not for Jane Cooper. She proceeds past the moment of tension into the inevitable dissolution in the next poem, "S. Eliason 66." In this case, one of the dissolutions in a portrait is the death and disappearance of the subjects of the painting:

> She is just leaving the room.
> He fades to a china cup.[9]

Subjects having neatly departed the scene, the painter herself, the actual process of creating the painting and the landscape in which the painting was created are all conflated into a brief and frenetic stanza. Once the reader is disoriented with this kaleidoscopic presentation, Dickinson and her life are reintroduced into the landscape, now occupying the same space as the painter's own mental processes:

> Velocity fraught with gold,
> with *menace of light,* atomic secrets—
> An aroused skin opens over the Great Plains.
> October leaves rain down.
>
> Corn in conflagration!
> The great retreats of the Civil War!
> Marriage in conflagration!

What's funny is that I remember the painting in Cooper's apartment, but I cannot remember where it hung. You would think it a riot of color, the trembling figures within inches of each other, the space between two bodies unbearably close, but the strange part is that it's the space and not the figures I remember. They are at either of end of the canvas, painted quite stiffly, she in "her Puritan white dress" and he "in his fiberboard suit." Between: that I remember. A field of luminous golden light, painted in swathes, smoothly, with white coming through. It's that immense space suspended that dominates the vision, crowds the figures themselves nearly out of the field of vision, echoes with all that was unsaid between the two, all that remains unsaid.

Perhaps the space also reflects the Iowa landscape in which Eliason was working, mirroring the private spaces in Dickinson's mind, the "desolation" of which Cooper spoke in her own life. The "marriage in conflagration" suddenly seems very ominous, looming very large—not merely Wadsworth's marriage itself, but the very idea of "marriage"—of joining between objects and people. The space between the two friends seems to endanger any possibility of it.

Cooper has a vision of integration past all the space and danger it entails:

> Years—an empty canvas.
> She scrawls across radiant space
>
> E . . . I . . . SON! *I made this.* The date.
> Name within name.

The space represents not only physical distance but time. One is tempted to misread "scrawl" as "crawl"—as the letters of Eliason's name are contained in Emily Dickinson's name, one word is contained in the other. There's suddenly something comforting about being sheathed, being contained—to live within another person. Cooper celebrates Eliason's transference here—from alienation to enveloping within the work of art, within Dickinson herself. She accomplishes this by the act of traveling across the distance between artist and art, by claiming it to her. The glyph "E . . . I . . . SON"—the scrawl across radiant space—and the italic of the painter finally speaking for herself, signing and dating her work, all become powerful moments of reconciliation with the separated being—such reconciliation not being a dissolution of one body into another, but the housing rather of one body *within* the other, that word "within" in the final line resting comfortably between the "names" of the two women so important to Jane Cooper.

She is thus able to find in language itself the space and elasticity to begin exploring the sound and spirit inherent in writing, the vowels and the way they open up spaces in the body. The relationship between an individual and the community and world around her becomes then not a space of alienation, but instead the space of possibility, the space of achieving the state of "within."

"Starting with a Line from Roethke," another of the withheld poems, demonstrates Cooper's far-ranging concern with sound and open spaces in the language. She moves in it from meditation to concrete observation, using the syllables themselves to create a wonderful music. The short twelve-line poem opens with four couplets that mirror each other:

To have the whole air!
To own, for the moment, nothing.

The purl of a wood-thrush winding down through the blazing
    afternoon.
The least flick of leaves.

Sunlight as energy
but diffused until it becomes the soft clang of poems

approaching from a great way off
out of the cave of the past . . .[10]

The vowels unfold into the air in the first couplet and echo into
space in the fourth couplet here. Between them couplets of un-
even line lengths. See how the long line sets up a series of long
vowel sounds and soft consonants, a wind through the natural
world that turns on the second short line and that delicious
"flick." The couplet after this reverses the strategy and introduces the unseen bell in the phrase "soft clang of poems."

After the sound plays itself through the "cave of the past"
and drifts away on the ellipse, Cooper closes the poem with a
penultimate couplet of exciting and sensual music (Cooper
pronounced the word "sexual" with a hard "k" sound), and
then a final couplet in which the still-unnamed bell literally
rings off across water. Not since Poe's "tintinnabulation" has a
bell rung itself through language as finely as the "soft clang" of
the unmentioned ocean buoy in the word "Tintagel" at the end
of this poem:

> Frida Kahlo's exuberant fruit,
> hacked open and sexual, or
>
> cliffs ringing with the calm off Tintagel.
> Calm off Tintagel.

The poem works sonically from the beginning, drawing the
sounds inside itself until the final enactment of ringing. The
text itself becomes a human body, breathing in and out, living
in space, no subject really, other than itself.

One of the most precious things about Cooper's poetic body
of work is that it really *is* a body. Not comprised of discrete

books published one after the other, punctuated by the occasional "new and selected" retrospective, Cooper's books instead accrete slowly, one after the other, each including work from the book before it, often revised subtly in pieces and places, three of her five books also including the prose essay discussed earlier.

Her poem "Waiting" is included in three of her five books, *Maps and Windows, Scaffolding* and *The Flashboat,* in three different versions.

The poems begins, in all three versions:

> My body knows it will never bear children.
> What can I say to my body now,
> this used violin?
> Every night it cries out strenuously
> from its secret cave.[11]

The body is at once extremely personal and utterly objectified—an object, even if a beautiful instrument, separate from the spirit's identity nonetheless. She goes on:

> Old body, old friend,
> why are you so unforgiving?
>
> Why are you so stiff and resistant
> clenched around empty space?
> An instrument is not a box.
>
> But suppose you are an empty box?
> Suppose you are like that famous wooden music hall in Troy,
>   New York,
> waiting to be torn down
> where the orchestras love to play?

She allows herself the ultimate question, the one the soul with all of its attendant anxieties about mortality and permanent cessation with the body's death never even allows itself to ask, the question a childless woman (or man!) approaching old age might wish to avoid: "But suppose you are an empty box . . . waiting to be torn down," though in the first version of the poem, the body cries out "desolately," while in the later versions of the poem, the body cries out "strenuously." Once more she asserts the sublimation of the human individual to the larger force of creation.

The first version of "Waiting," published in *Maps and Windows* in 1974, ends with the couplet:

> Let compassion breathe in and out of you
> filling you with poems[12]

By 1984's *Scaffolding,* Cooper opts for something a little more essential, a little closer to the source of poetry than the actual word "poems," and closes the poem like this:

> Let compassion breathe in and out of you
> filling you, singing[13]

But when Cooper revises all of her earlier work, restoring many previously unpublished poems in *The Flashboat: Poems Collected and Reclaimed,* she revisits "Waiting" once again. This time, instead of seeing "singing" as the reification of "poems," she sees the whole motion of breath as a process, an action unto itself that doesn't end, as in "work, the starry waters" in the poem "The Flashboat." Instead of a mere receptacle being filled, the body itself becomes the instrument of compassion—she ends the poem like this:

> Let compassion breathe in and out of you,
> breathe in and out of you

NOTES

1. Jane Cooper, *The Flashboat* (New York: W. W. Norton & Company, 2000), 202.
2. Ibid., 57.
3. Ibid., 58.
4. Ibid., 101.
5. Ibid., 208.
6. Ibid., 144.
7. Ibid., 125.
8. Ibid., 146.
9. Ibid., 147.

10. Ibid., 150.

11. Ibid., 140.

12. Jane Cooper, *Maps and Windows* (New York: Macmillan Publishing, 1974), 27.

13. Jane Cooper, *Scaffolding* (London: Anvil Press Poetry, 1984), 90.

The Guardian of the
Gates of Paradise

I wish I could say my sense of alienation from the English language taught me how to torque it, how to make a poetic line.
For a long while it has been the individual line I was most interested in, usually to the detriment of the stanza, or even the
architecture of the poem as a whole. I wanted to make it queer,
to make it sing; in a sense I wanted for it to be pure music without context of the surrounding poem. On the other hand, as a
Muslim in America, a South Asian, part Arab and all strange, I
found myself desperate to narrate, express, harangue.

Agha Shahid Ali's poetry traveled a trajectory throughout his
life from sense to sound. Though always musical, his earlier
books were grounded in confessional experience and narrative,
but moved book by book as if spoken by an angel with a forked
tongue: pure strangeness and pure lucidity at once, textural
music and linear narrative both. *The Nostalgist's Map of America* is
probably his hinge moment; the narrative of a road trip across
the country coupled with a retelling of that myth of crazy love,
Layla and Majnoon, marked a stark departure from free verse
into the various forms that Shahid worked in throughout the
last three books he published. Form, for Shahid, was less about
stricture and more about detecting some shape that lingered in
the formlessness of sound in a poem. It was like the act of naming constellations, first seeing those unshaped frames of light.

Ali said something very interesting about the ghazal, likening
it to something that was happening in Modernist poetry: "When
my students ask about a poem such as *The Waste Land*—How
does it hold together?—I suggest a more compelling approach:
How does it *not* hold together?"[1]

Indeed, for some of us our lives do not hold together. The disparate parts do not find a thematic unity. How can one make art to describe a life like this? Interestingly, the question has added significance to the Muslim artist, as classical Islamic art eschews representation, and also eschews a sense of the artistic production (book, painting, building) as an object with senses of either linearity or completeness. Man, after all, is *not* the measure of all things.

There was a language I spoke but another language with which I tried to write. In a sense it was the language I was trying to write with that was closer to my heart—a language that wouldn't fly in daily life, couldn't be used to buy the groceries, check books and videos out from the library, pick up the mail and send packages. There was also, for me, an anxiety about the vocabulary of images: how could I use poetically a metaphor or image for which potential readers might have no cultural referents at all?

In Ali's poem "Dear Shahid," he imagines a friend in war-torn Kashmir writing to him about the condition of life and bodies. The image of a country without peace is told in the metaphors of modern technology—radios and televisions being smashed by the soldiers—and the ultimate demonstration of barbarism is that the post office is no longer delivering mail. Poetry, however, becomes a way of expressing those hopes for peace—in fact, the unnamed correspondent finds a letter to Ali in the abandoned post office and includes it in the envelope with the note that we, the readers, are perusing.

At the heart of this short five-paragraph poem is the story of two young men, both affected violently by the war. Rizwan, a friend of the narrator's, named after the mythic guardian of the gates of paradise, has been killed. The second young man—a stranger—has had the webs of his hands cut during torture. The tales of these two, one an intimate and the other a stranger, come to stand for all the violence perpetuated against bodies in a time of war, and the brutality of war itself as compared to the boons of peace, the ordinary, small parts of our daily lives like receiving the mail or listening to the radio. The correspondent is desperate to hold on to this quotidian life—in the midst of his recounting the story of the torture of the second young man, he interrupts himself like so:

> Yesterday at Hideout Café (everyone there asks about you), a doctor—who had just treated a sixteen-year-old boy released from an interrogation center—said: I want to ask the fortune-tellers: Did anything in his line of Fate reveal that the webs of his hand would be cut with a knife?"[2]

Through the interruptions we come to see the full texture of the experience of the individual body in a culture divided by war—though the news is dire and political, the social nature of the individual relationship always also still exists. The hands, cut violently here, return as a prayer in the closing image: "We are waiting for the almond blossoms. And, if God wills, O! those days of peace when we all were in love and the rain was in our hands wherever we went."

The image of the rain in the hands is so soothing, so lovely, compared to the lancing image of the webs of the hands sliced, but it mirrors also an image in the first paragraph of men forced to stand all night barefoot in snow. There is the tenderest of motions back and forth within the small prose text; it is itself an imagined missive, addressed to the man who is writing it himself. The lost letter with the text becomes a cipher for loneliness and alienation, but also the sign of hope: it has been sent—the poem has been written—after all, against the odds.

Like his friend James Merrill, whose poem "Charles on Fire," with its saturation of nautical imagery, he admired very much, Ali was interested in building a conceit in a poem and then exploring every possible metaphor associated with it. In his poem "Resume," he uses the language of business in a poem about a speaker who wants to achieve union with the condition of water, that is to say eternity. "I / an applicant / to the water's green offices / sign my name above a thin horizon," the poem opens.[3] To him, the manifestations of the divine on Earth, temples and mosques, are "postscripts on God." The speaker wants more than these mere reflections, but unfortunately for him, "those who promised / to recommend me // place the moon's blank sheets / in my hands unsigned."

The speaker is left with only "xeroxed rumors" as the "clerk of climates" tears up his forms and tells him, "no opening he says / no vacant reflection." The speaker is given only the ghost of a chance, which he jumps at: "Maybe he says Maybe—and I say Yes." He is invited then to join the water's offices, not completely, but at the most entry-level position: "I the secretary of memory / in chambers of weeds // the water's breathless bureaucracy." Ultimately, Ali certainly relishes the world-play and game-play of the conceit, but its purpose is not frivolous; he uses it to turn all the screws and increase the emotional tension of the speaker's search.

The sometimes over-performance of narrative voice in these poems is not really melodramatic the way an American ear might hear it, but rather is characteristic of that baroque and nearly overwrought sense of the poetic sublime that is the norm in Urdu poetry. In a sequence of poems entitled "From Amherst to Kashmir," Ali tells the story of accompanying his mother's body back to India for burial during the month of Muhurram, the first month of the Muslim calendar, but also commemorated by Shi'a Muslims as the month of mourning, in which Hussain, grandson of the prophet and spiritual leader of the Shi'a at the time, was killed by the ruling caliph, along with much of his extended family. In the poems, he tries to link the historical story of Karbala, the place Hussain was killed, with his grief at losing his mother. In fact, throughout the sequence—Zainab's loss of her brother Hussain at Karbala, Ali's mother's identification with Zainab's grief, Ali's own grief at the passing of famed ghazal singer Bhegum Akhtar (a grief he revisits in poem after poem throughout his career)—multiple losses are conflated with the overarching loss Ali feels at the passing of his mother.

Unlike his mother, who was able to make her grief a part of her daily experience, the poet is nearly overcome by it: "But for me, I who of passion / always make a holocaust, will there be a summer of peace?"[4] As the month of mourning commences and Ali begins his journey back to Kashmir, there is no peace offered: "It is Muharram again. / Of God there is no sign. / Mother, / you are 'the breath drawn after every line.'" Throughout the ensuing poems—pantoums, sapphic stanzas, ghazals and villanelles—lines of Zainab's lament, translated as the second part of the sequence, are sprinkled through, calling to mind the role of grief in Shi'a culture—a daily fact of life that is supposed to suffuse one's awareness of the present moment. It is a son's separation from a mother, to be sure, but also, in the Sufi interpretation, the individual soul weeping at his isolation from the Divine.

In "Film *Bhajan* Found on a 78 RPM," the seventh poem in the series, Ali experiments with dispensing with punctuation in order to foreground the experience of the tumble of feelings which accompany grief. "Dark god shine on me you're all I have left / nothing else blue god you are all I have," he opens.[5] This elimination of commas and eschewing of midline caesurae or other cues to a separation of thoughts finds a later flowering in the work of Reetika Vazirani. There also, the sense of the claustrophobia and immediacy of intense emotions is heightened. Interestingly, the blue god to whom Shahid is praying here is not Allah but Krishna: "Dark god you are all you are all I have," closes the poem. "Swear only swear I am yours I am yours."

The poet somehow doesn't need to "explain anything"— everything of import is packed into the poem, its form and shape carrying any additional information not told in it. The poem "Srinagar Airport" bears an epigraph, "There is no god but God," a rendering of the Arabic line *la-ilaha-il-Allah*. In sapphic stanzas, Ali tells of the arrival in Kashmir, using the final truncated line to imitate the speechlessness of the situation: "Even they are here speechless, weeping, / those of passion // never made a holocaust."[6]

Often using the truncated fourth line of the sapphic to break the stanza in a critical place, Ali plays on the upper- and lowercase gods in the penultimate and final stanzas: "She is / farther than any // god today and nearer than any god. And / God? He's farther, farther from us, forever / far." His final lines repeat a similarly truncated version of the epigraph, cut with devastating effect: "We lift the shrine. The women break into / *There is no god but.*"

However, lest one think that for the poet it is a simple matter of defying and denying divinity in anger at loss, the immediately following poem in the sequence is entitled (uppercase) "God," thus completing the truncated bit of the final sapphic stanza of the previous poem and moving into a rhythmic and melodious villanelle, though with a dark and dour refrain: "God then is only the final assassin."[7]

Ali is unable, or unwilling, to leave the line—and thus the sentiment—well enough alone. He continues to riff on this, and on the villanelle's second refrain, which also contains a traditional Quranic opening: "'In the Name of the Merciful' let night begin." As he travels through his lament at the actual burial, he comes to two new and visceral versions of the refrain, "God is the only, the only assassin," and "In no one's name but hers I let night begin."

The Urdu and Arabic forms, including the ghazal, Ali worked in lend themselves to this treatment of the line as a unit of poetry itself, a treatment that has retreated somewhat in new forms of Western poetry that eschew meter as a primary building block of individual lines. In particular, when the typical free verse poem, whether it uses meter or not, is written in short, enjambed lines, one finds a harder time of it actually hearing the music of a line. In all of Ali's poetry, one really hears the line quoted against space, whether the unrhymed free verse couplets of his earlier books, or the strictly formal schemes of his later work, including monostichic verse and a few one-line poems which Shahid always took delight in reciting. When he read his own "On Hearing a Lover Not Seen for Twenty Years Has Attempted Suicide," he always deliciously declaimed the poem's single line: "I suspect it was over me."[8] The form of the one-line poem could be as pathos inducing as it was humorous though. He adored (and frequently performed) Merwin's "Epitaph": "o but who would I show it to."

The ghazal, championed by Ali, lends itself to bridging the gap between the line as an individual expulsion of poetic energy, and the line as a part of the mosaic which builds a formal arrangement of an individual poem. In *Call Me Ishmael Tonight,* his magnificent final book, Ali creates poems riffing on lines from many poets he loves, including W. S. Merwin, Daniel Hall, Galway Kinnell, Mark Strand and Michael Palmer. In "For You," he writes to Palmer, "Because in this dialect the eyes are crossed or quartz, / A STATUE A RAZOR A FACT I exclaim for you," and later in the signature couplet he uses both Palmer's name and his own: "God's dropped the scales. Whose wings will cover me, Michael? / Don't pronounce the sentence Shahid over-came for you."[9]

Indeed, the passage of energy through a poem or through a body brings up the question of both the restraint and release of that energy, but also of both the poem's end and the body's end, that is to say: its death. Many of the ghazals in his last book were written while Ali was undergoing treatment for cancer. He confronts his own mortality and his complex feelings toward God in various lines. "Father of Clay, this is Shahid: I am become flesh— / No spirit dusts or will itself redeem about me."[10]

Certainly, above all, the ghazal is a community form, a per-formed form. Its integrity is in sound and in inventiveness. He truly expanded the sense of poetic community by bringing the form into English, introducing it into countless teaching an-thologies and an anthology he edited himself entitled *Ravishing Disunities*. He was, after all, interested in the beauty of grief, of entropy, of things that did not hold together. The line or couplet in the form of a ghazal has a delirious and rapturous relationship to the architecture of a poem entire—individual couplets can be rearranged, added, deleted, without changing the poem as a whole. In this sense, like the calligraphy, architecture and geo-metric patterns of Islamic arts, it is an object loved for its formal properties, loved for its quick switches in tone, from coolness, to humor, to profundity, characterized in its nature—since a refrain repeats throughout the poem—by plumbing multiple meanings, textures and contexts from a single word or phrase. In his ghazal "Forever," he demonstrates this scintillating shift of moods and tones across the poem. Here are four various couplets:

> On the gibbet Hallaj cried *I am the Truth.*
> In this universe one dies a plaintive forever.
>
> When parents fall in love with those blond assassins,
> their children sign up for Western Civ forever.
>
> The Hangman washes his hands, puts his son to sleep.
> But for whom, come dawn, he's decisive forever?
>
> You've forgiven everyone Shahid, even God—
> Then how could someone like you not live forever?[11]

If the ghazal at first seems a form of dissolution, one only has to see exile—as Mahmoud Darwish did, as Ali did—as a form of homeland to sense its beauty. In the earlier version of his ghazal "Arabic," Ali wrote, "When Lorca died, they left the balconies open and saw: / his *qasidas* braided, on the horizon, into knots of Arabic."[12] When he revisited the ghazal and rewrote its lines in a later version, he found Lorca's Arabic forms not to be torqued and tied tightly into knots but rather as an integral component of his existence: "When Lorca died, they left the balconies open and saw / on the sea his *qasidas* stitched seamless in Arabic."[13]

Ali was hailed as being part of a formalist trend in poetry, but it was an affiliation he did not embrace: "I love forms, but I do not wish to come across as some kind of formalist. I am not, certainly not, the neo-kind who wishes to save Western Civilization—with meters and rhymes!"[14] In the end, his interest in strict form did not stem from any conservative instinct—rather, it was profoundly revolutionary. Writing in these complicated forms—and for this poet, the more complicated, the better—most of which, like the canzone, the ghazal and the sapphic stanza, were invented in different historical periods, and for languages other than English—was his way of twisting the language into complicated poses—reminiscent of yoga asanas, and like the asanas, these "poses" of language were not performed to create a visual (or linguistic) sense of "beauty," but rather with the aim of thus accessing the inner, unstable spirit. In this way, Ali worked in a Sufi tradition, attempting, through extreme "form," rhyme schemes, repetitions, metrical contortions—to reach the state of inspired ecstasy—a moment of pure feeling *without* senses.

So a form, though caught in the binds of restraint, is not about the stilling of energy but about the shaping and releasing of energy. It is, as Mark Doty has argued, a gesture against death. Sense and sound move dangerously against one another within the framework of the line and the couplet in Ali's work. I may find my own answer there.

In the end,

Shahid won't let Death make of Love a ruin of light.[15]

1. Agha Shahid Ali, "Ghazal: The Charms of a Considered Disunity," in *The Practice of Poetry,* ed. Robin Behn and Chase Twichell (New York: Harper Paperbacks, 1992), 205.

2. Agha Shahid Ali, *The Veiled Suite* (New York: W. W. Norton & Company, 2009), 194.

3. Ibid., 152.

4. Ibid., 258.

5. Ibid., 266.

6. Ibid., 267.

7. Ibid., 269.

8. Ibid., 295.

9. Ibid., 327.

10. Ibid., 354.

11. Ibid., 369.

12. Ibid., 225.

13. Ibid., 372.

14. Agha Shahid Ali, "The Ghazal in America: May I?," in *After New Formalism,* ed. Annie Finch (Oregon: Story Line Press, 1999), 129.

15. Ali, *Veiled Suite,* 364.

In the Hurricane's Eye

On Mahmoud Darwish

When Jane Cooper confronted the fact that the war had become, for her, a lens through which to write of a desolation more personal, she engaged a struggle in artistic production that seems peculiarly American. Contemporary poets in the U.S. seem to find themselves suspended between Walt Whitman—sprawling, public, ecstatic—and Emily Dickinson—hermetic, interior, controlled. Whether one chooses a side or works at fusing the opposing impulses, one is still caught in the idea of a binary.

In that sense, Mahmoud Darwish, a Palestinian poet who spent most of his life in exile outside the borders of Palestine, becomes an important poet for the developing conscience of twenty-first-century America.

The three books collected in *The Butterfly's Burden* were all written and published after Darwish's 1997 return to Palestine after twenty-four years in exile, first in Lebanon, then Libya, and finally France. Though Darwish has nearly always been read through a political lens (and Cooper, somewhat ironically, always read apolitically), in an interview given in 1995, he himself claimed exactly the opposite for himself and his work: "History cannot be reduced to a compensation for the lost geography. It's also a place of observation between shadows, between the self and the Other, known in more complex human ways . . . Is it just an aesthetic trick, simple gesture? Or is it that despair seizes the body? The response is of no importance. The essential thing is that I found a great lyric capacity and a passage from the relative to the absolute. An opening in which I inscribe the national into the universal, that Palestine is not limited to Palestine, but it has established its aesthetic legitimacy in a human realm much vaster."[1]

"Let's go as we are," the first poem in "The Stranger's Bed" opens, seeming to invite a break from opposition, a break from strife: "soon there will be a new present for us. / If you look back you will see only / the exile of your looking back."[2] The notion of exile is not political here, has nothing to do with the "lost geography" of which Darwish spoke of above, but is a human condition; Like Cooper's "desolation," it is a condition of loss beyond the political, a loss, Darwish seems to say, that a political healing will not be able to reconcile. There is some resignation here to be sure—"Our time wasn't enough to grow old to-gether / to walk wearily to the cinema / to witness the end of Athens's war with her neighbors / and to see the banquet of peace between Rome and Carthage / about to happen"—but an awareness that the solutions of community and polity will be able to resuscitate neither the individual nor the lost "home-land": "No cultural solutions for existential concerns / . . . / Wherever you go my sky / is real."

The poems, though discrete, lock themselves in the mind of the reader by repeating both abstract concepts—peace, exile, poetry, loneliness—and concrete objects and images—wheat, silk, hands, dust, birds. One gets the feeling of being submerged in a consciousness, almost as if the poems were a stream without clear beginnings or endings. If such a comparison tips Darwish to the more "Whitmanesque," in an American vocabulary, the poems themselves remain gorgeously elusive, at their core purely "Dickinsonian" in both their clever rhythmic structures and in their strangely nocturnal energies.

Many of Darwish's quotidian observances are of things from afar, things that are impossible to know: "There's a love passing through us, / without us noticing, / and neither it knows nor do we know / why a rose in an ancient wall makes us fugitives / and why a girl at the bus stop cries: / Nothing, nothing more / than a bee passing through my blood . . ."[3] The reader is so entranced by the examples and imagery Darwish uses to de-scribe the feeling of not understanding love that he nearly misses the realization that it wasn't love at all moving through the blood, but another object entirely, the bee. One experiences the loss within the physical lines of the poetry itself, moving through the poem.

Darwish does not want to escape into the purely abstract; he always marries it tightly to very physical and real conditions. It is almost as if to write symbolically or metaphorically becomes another form of exile, another form of separation from the human and the real. He muses to a lover, "A real country, not a metaphor, your arms / around me . . . over there by the holy book / or right here. Who of us said: Language / might preserve the land from the plight / of absence if poetry wins?"[4]

It's the "right here" that resonates—the lovers' arms become a place more permanent, more actual, more real that the holy book, than "Language," than the "poetry" that would "preserve the land from the plight / of absence." When physical bodies are shared, Darwish offers, exile evaporates. It took a man coming home after very real "exile" to write poems like this, though it's important to add, sometimes home is not home. Darwish came back to Ramallah, but the village in which he was born and raised, Birweh, no longer exists—it is one of those that was cleared and razed in the war of 1948. "The night sits wherever you are," he writes in a subsequent poem, alluding to the true secret knowledge of one permanently exiled, not that he will never have a home again, but that any place, any place at all, holds the possibility of becoming a home.

For Darwish, much of this "homing in" comes from human interactions, experiences of love with other people. He writes, "in our bodies / a heaven and earth embrace" and "Night / in the covenant of night, crawling in my body."[5] Not only are the bodies twinned in each other, a single unit, but "Night" can lie within itself, an object inside the same object, the ultimate in intimacy. He seems to suggest there is no possibility for reconciliation unless the two strangers meet each other and recognize one another in the other. No possibility without such means, of course, that every possibility for reconciliation does exist: "Go to the sea then, man, west of your book, / and dive lightly, lightly as if you were carrying / yourself at birth in two waves, / you'll find a wetland forest and a green sky / of water, then dive lightly / lightly as if you were nothing in anything, / and you'll find us together . . . / we are one in two / We need to see how we were here."[6]

It's a most personal mourning, and Darwish seems very conscious of poetry's role in trying to create a reality in which the self can authentically actualize itself: "Of night, I love the beginning, when you two come together / hand in hand, and bit by bit embrace me one section at a time."[7] The stakes, though, are high for him; he knows poetry is not mere play or ecstatic utterance, and though he seems to feel sometimes a mere instrument for greater breath, he has great faith in his work as a craftsman: "But the flute should be patient / and polish a sonnet, when you two descend on me . . . it chooses me as a threshold // of Poetry." It's a beautiful thing to think of the poet's human sensing body as a "threshold" that poetry will cross, from wordlessness into this world, and "what flows from you," he says, "is 'I' the free and kind."

"A State of Siege," one of Darwish's book-length poems, though written during the events of the siege of Ramallah, focuses neither on political polemic, nor on autobiographical confessional, but is an intensely personal lyric response in a language that really has no equivalent ("yet," one hopes) in the American idiom. "Don't trust the poem," Darwish writes, "this daughter of absence, / she's neither speculation / nor intellect, / she's chasm's sense."[8] Though at the same time, he knows poetry is *real:* "I wrote twenty lines about love / and imagined / this siege / has withdrawn twenty meters!"[9] The key here is that the poem which caused the siege's withdrawal (even if only in the imagination of the poet) was a poem of love. Earlier he writes, "This siege will extend until we teach our enemies / paradigms of our Jahili poetry."[10]

One of the paradigms in Darwish's work is the motion of the "relative to the Absolute," as he stated in the interview quoted above—more specifically, the motion of an abstract against a very particular or quotidian: "Here, by the downslope of hills, facing the sunset / and time's muzzle," he opens the long poem. If in a Darwish poem one feels always lost because one never gets the simple sunset without "time's muzzle," he takes care of you in reverse—you'll never get dropped into the abstraction of time's muzzle without the actual sunset there to anchor you. Things are all so unreal they have to imagine even themselves: "life with its shortcomings, / hosts neighboring stars / that are timeless . . . / and immigrant clouds / that are placeless. / And life here / wonders: / How do we bring it back to life!" The pronouns teach you a lesson here, life wondering how to bring something to life.

The epic and lyric collide not only in Darwish's form, but also in the content of the poems: "Pain / is: that a housewife doesn't hang up her clothesline / in the morning, and that she's satisfied with this flag's cleanliness." When people turn away from the local, the small elements of their lives, he seems to say, they lose any ability to see the poetry, the ineffable, the spiritual in the world: "The soldiers measure the distance between being / and nonbeing / with a tank's scope . . ." The oppressed, on the other hand, the alienated, the unhomed, have nothing left but their spiritual resources: "We measure the distance between our bodies / and mortar shells . . . with the sixth sense." It is interesting to note here that the soldiers are in possession of spiritual material ("being and nonbeing") but do not have the resources to comprehend them, while the speaker and his comrades have the coarse material of destruction to contend with and only the tools of ineffability with which to do so.

Throughout the long sequence on the siege, Darwish meditates on the actual events, describes personal responses to them and also tries to enact, in poetic form, the peculiar atmosphere, frequently along the way displaying a clever wit and humor, even comedy, rarely seen in his more earnest lyric works that frame this poem in the collection. For example, in writing about the strange unfolding of time during a siege: "Whenever yesterday arrives, I tell it: / Our appointment is not today, so go away / and come back tomorrow!"[11]

You are always in a dream, reading Darwish, reading between the ephemeral and the absolute, the "person" himself and the larger universe (sometimes symbolically represented as "poetry") often dissolving into each other. At one point in the poem, Darwish (likely tired of being interpreted as a "political writer") fires off a little barb, that—true to Darwish form—dissolves from tartness into poetry: "Do not interpret my words / with a teaspoon or a bird snare! / My speech besieges me in sleep, / my speech that I have not yet said, / it writes me then leaves me searching / for the remnants of my sleep . . ."[12] He's writing perhaps of an actual siege in the world, but in his poetic imagination he is under siege by his own speech; it's not a speech that kills him but a speech that "writes" him; "sleep," the town in which he was supposed to be protected, is in tatters around him. "Let the endless complete its infinite chores," he writes, "As for me I'll whisper to the shadow: If / the history of the place were less crowded / our eulogies to the topography of / poplar trees . . . would've been more!"

Studded with small lyric moments, testy vociferations, desperate pleadings and darkly philosophical epigrams, the sequence imitates the curious counterpoint of boredom and terror inherent in the days passed during a siege: "This siege will extend until / the besieger feels, like the besieged, / that boredom / is a human trait." Later, in a section that addresses various abstracts—the poet, poetry, prose—Darwish requests, "(To poetry): Besiege your siege." The sequence ends in a beautiful and lyrically cadenced outburst of pure lyric, the poet singing for his life, singing for the end of the siege, singing for peace.

Joudah chooses not to translate the wonderful Arabic word for peace, "salaam," letting instead its vowels do the work. Once more in the closing motion of the poem-sequence, Darwish opts for the most human of feelings rather than mere political speech: "Salaam is two enemies longing, each separately / to yawn on boredom's sidewalk // Salaam is two lovers moaning to bathe / in moonlight."[13] When he does seem to tilt to the political it actually sounds more like pure love poetry: "Salaam is the apology of the might to the one / with weaker weapons and stronger range // Salaam is the sword breaking in front of natural / beauty, where dew smelts the iron."

In the final collected book of *The Butterfly's Burden*, "Don't Apologize for What You've Done," Darwish seems to move to a very personal, even conversational tone. Perhaps it was the extreme concision and tight compression of the lyrics of "A State of Siege" that then allowed the luxurious flowering of voice in the final book, the feast after the fast, as it were. Darwish returns home in "The Stranger's Bed," then realizes that even home is not always home in "A State of Siege," and so in "Don't Apologize" he passes into a third awareness.

Appropriately he uses Lorca as one of the epigraphs: "And

now, I am not I / and the house is not my house," although in the Arabic translation of Lorca, the negation comes first, something like: "And neither am I, I / nor the house, my house." The sense of alienation is somewhat profounder in the Arabic, and this desire to place oneself in the midst of alienation pervades the book.

The blurring of boundaries between self and the larger universe around seems slowed down here, even absent. The absolute or universal slides off the original, doesn't stick: "Cadence chooses me, it chokes on me / I am the violin's regurgitant flow, and not its player."[14] This relationship between poet and poem is so different from the earlier expression of the flute that polishes the sonnet. While he still has faith in the powers of poetry to restore—"Whenever I listen to the stone I hear / the cooing of a white pigeon"—a new despair has entered: "I am still here / but you won't return as you were when I left you / you won't return and I won't return." The poetry, or "cadence," that would have so seamlessly before integrated with the poet's consciousness, remains something exterior here, even undesired. Or is it the poet himself that is now undesired by poetry: "cadence completes its cycle / and chokes on me . . ."

Darwish seems to move, in this section, from the abstracted and symbolic into concrete and real situations, the closest he has come to a straight poetry of narration. For example, in "Nothing Pleases Me": "Nothing pleases me / the traveler on the bus says—Not the radio / or the morning newspaper, nor the citadels on the hills."[15] But don't be tricked—it is still Darwish with all his hallmarks—the negotiation between the material world and the intangible spiritual world, the slipperiness of boundaries between awareness, the quick motion between plain narrative and deliciously mysterious lyric; after the traveler confesses his existential crisis, others on the bus join in, first a woman with her practical complaint, "I guided my son to my grave, / he liked it and slept there, without saying goodbye," and then the poem takes its left turn into strangeness with the student who confesses, "I studied archeology but didn't / find identity in stone. Am I / really me?" and the soldier (perhaps one of those from "A State of Siege" who found themselves unable to resolve the difference between being and unbeing?) who says, "I always besiege a shot / besieging me." Though the group refuses in a panic to depart the bus as it approaches the last stop, the weary speaker admits, "Let me off here. I am / like them, nothing pleases me, but I'm worn out / from travel."

With this release, then, Darwish assembles a beautiful final section of domestic scenes, poetic exploration, philosophical music and spiritual vision. He brings all of his intense energies to bear in the daily and material world, examining the nature of history by way of an imaginary conversation in an abandoned theater, channeling Yannis Ritsos in Neruda's house, or talking poignantly about the exile of a Kurdish friend in terms both tender—"the winds have no suitcases, and no job for dust"—and fierce—"come here you son of a bitch and let's beat this night's / drum until we awaken the dead."

Something very brief must be said about Darwish's line break. He breaks it not with the traditional prosody of the poetic line or even with breath, but seemingly as free verse poets often do, for the most dramatic impact, though in Darwish it is often used as a de-centering strategy. For example, in "Nothing Pleases Me," quoted above, lines break not on nouns but on phrases like "am I" and "didn't find." The de-centered sense, a sense of wandering within the poem itself, is thus heightened.

For too long, poetry—at least American poetry—been stuck between false poles, feeling the need to make a choice between personal and political, between accessible and hermetic, between community orientation and self-orientation. We might take notice of what Fady Joudah writes of Darwish: "Translation should, as Darwish suggests, become more than a new poem in another language, it should expend into that language new vastness."[16]

NOTES

1. Mahmoud Darwish, *La Palestine comme métaphore,* translated from the Arabic by Simone Bitton and Elias Sanbar (Paris: Sinbad, 1997), 125–26. Excerpt translated from the French by Kazim Ali.

2. Mahmoud Darwish, *The Butterfly's Burden,* trans. Fady Joudah (Port Townsend, WA: Copper Canyon Press, 2007), 5.

3. Ibid., 15.
4. Ibid., 21.
5. Ibid., 23.
6. Ibid., 27.
7. Ibid., 33.
8. Ibid., 167.
9. Ibid., 151.
10. Ibid., 143.
11. Ibid., 127.
12. Ibid., 129.
13. Ibid., 171.
14. Ibid., 179.
15. Ibid., 247.
16. Fady Joudah, introduction to *The Butterfly's Burden,* by Mahmoud Darwish (Port Townsend, WA: Copper Canyon Press, 2007), xv.

Poetry and Music

The instruments I love the most are the ones that sound so human—a cello, the English horn, the oboe. I like to hear the drummer's fingers move across the drum, or the metallic noise of a callous dragging across a guitar string.

Similarly, the voices I love the most are the ones that fail—a singer like Björk reaching a very low note, or Ani DiFranco out of breath or laughing while she sings, or Yoko Ono's voice breaking on notes from "Goodbye Sadness."

It seems to me that poetry and music share the main affinity of working against silence. In poetry, the language works against silence, but also the subject or content of the poem must modulate against the unsaid part.

George Braque wrote, of the appeal of a vase as a compositional object to Cubist painters, "The vase gives form to emptiness as music gives to silence." May I swerve from the statement and go to the metaphor?

Music has always been equally about the tones and the spaces between them. Is it possible for one note to offer emotional content? I believe it is. In yoga, breath is considered the core of practice. In my own Muslim upbringing I was told a saying of one of the imams: "God is closer to you than your own breath." I wonder what lives between the inhale and the exhale?

Scientists tell us that the universe made a sound in the beginning. It is as likely as any other that the sound was OM. What if the universe still echoes from that first sound? By gauging the light of very distant stars, it is now also known that the speed of the universe is not, as was previously believed, constant. Stars continue to accelerate *away* from us. Assuming both the expansion and contraction are equal, we are not yet even halfway through the life of the universe.

A comforting thought in the uncertain world.

That music can define silence was probably most radically demonstrated by John Cage in his *4'33"*, but Morton Feldman actually worked through the silence, positioning individual notes sometimes, building phrases and sounds that worked against a purely melodic line, the kind that uses mathematical chord progressions, a line or theme one can predict the outcome of, once one gets hold of it aurally—or, as they say, "hum along." I think particularly of Feldman's haunting *Rothko Chapel,* chilling soundscapes that wash over the listener in an evocation of Rothko's hauntingly *not*-minimalist paintings.

When we think of music in poetry, we might most often think about sound, rhythm, meter, assonance and repetition. I'm after something else: a music of the sentence, a music in the way a thought works.

Here's a stanza from Olga Broumas's collaboration with T Begley, entitled *Sappho's Gymnasium:*

> Lord let me all I can wild cherry
> I'm dazed all my ways of arriving bear tracks
> failure of being torn to pieces is me
> mumbling anxiety and I love my heart
> I do each day lightly suffering desire
> for kindness vividly today
> idiot red unselfish green blue threadbare of cloud
> outside the labyrinth imagining my life[1]

Here is a luscious unbraiding of syntactic relationships. It would be wrong to even go back to the rubric of parts of speech to try to assign relationships here. (For example: can "wild cherry" in the first line function as a verb? Can we put commas in the fifth line to return it to grammatical sense?) Rather, the intent here is musical sense—the poem is "about" something the way music has a subject.

Language is always representational to me, even if the writer's goal is to uncouple the representation that seems to be the starting point. Is music representational? When Stravinsky wrote about the "fire-bird," in what ways did he write the "fire"? Similarly, how did Mussorgsky spell "mountain" or Feldman describe Rothko? We would need the vocabulary of composers and the knowledge of theory to explain it.

If Broumas and Begley work in the lyric or ecstatic mode of music, then Susan Howe can be called a narrative poet of this mode. She works from story, and is perhaps interested rhythmically not in this mellifluous gorgeousness, but in a starker, more syncopated line, more haunted, more filled with silences. Here is a small piece of the first poem in "Pythagorean Silence" from her book *Europe of Trusts:*

> age of earth and us all chattering
>
> a sentence or character
> suddenly
>
> steps out to seek for truth fails
> falls
>
> into a stream of ink Sequence
> trails off
>
> must go on
>
> waving fables and faces War
> doings of the war
>
> manoeuvering between points
> between
>
> any two points which is
> what we want[2]

Her couplets somewhat imitate Dickinsonian prosody, the second line a beat or two shorter than the one before. Each shorter and truncated line also speaks three ways: to the phrase before it, to the phrase after it and to the silence surrounding it. Once the poem does stutter: "must go on." As with much of Howe's work, these poems are performative as *material*—both sonically as language and spatially on the page—but also political in the way they treat silence and give voice to those silenced by history. As Howe says in the prefatory essay to the volume, "I wish I could tender lift from the dark side of history, voices that are anonymous, slighted—inarticulate."[3]

Broumas and Begley's music shows the exciting possibility of loss in the erotic fluidity of language and language systems; Howe's is a darker prophetic voice of how language has functioned in history—an obscurer, a mistranslator, an apologist for imperial war.

These poets are engaged—beyond their compelling subject matter, and from very different aesthetic positions—in foregrounding the performance of language within the poem.

Jean Valentine works with a similar attention to syntax and silence, but perhaps without the foregrounding of the language as material.

Here's the first of Valentine's "Two Poems for Matthew Shepard" from her collection *Door in the Mountain: New and Collected Poems:*

> But what about the blue dory—the soul
>
> —*Thief the sun Thief the rain*
>
> Into love
> the size of a silver dollar
> [the soul] disappeared
> to a pencil point then
> nothing.
>   Left
> his nails
> and his hair.[4]

In this poem, the lack of punctuation in the initial question, the line in italics, the change in lineation, the bracketing of "the soul," the tabbed word, each subsequently works against the previous formal outlay of the poem. The soul appears in it, softly and without warning—the question isn't answered. The final sentence omits the subject, "[the soul]" having already departed.

What could happen to poetry if we left the mathematical systems, the tonal registers—the way Broumas, Begley, Howe and Valentine do?

Music, like poetry, is composed. A classical composer (or a pop-music songwriter) will work within a given mode, given sets of notes, keys. Even twelve-tone composers like Schoenberg and

Webern worked within systems. Even Cage and Feldman, revolutionary and immense, were interested in systems.

What happens to music when it leaves the system? Yoko Ono, Alice Coltrane and Sheila Chandra are three contemporary musicians whose work departs from the known into the territory that Broumas, Begley, Howe and Valentine mine in words, a place where silence, the individual's own actual sound (in Coltrane's case her instrument, but for Chandra and Ono the human voice) and the universe of emotion govern what music is, not the mathematics of the system.

Ono's voice is a sculptural object. In a masterwork of the early seventies, "Fly," Ono modulates a single note dropping out of sung registers into the throat for twenty-two minutes. The piece is the soundtrack for her film of the same name in which a woman's naked body is treated as a vast landscape for a single fly.

Coltrane works her organ and harp off the page. Ornette Coleman, also a collaborator of Ono's, actually sat and transcribed Coltrane's performance of "Universal Consciousness" so that other musicians might learn the music.

Sheila Chandra, in her *ABoneCroneDrone* series, shows that a single note carries immense emotional weight on its own, but there is really no such thing as a "single note." Each one carries under it a harmonic series (mathematically plottable) of numerous other notes.

The source of the art supersedes the limitations of the medium itself. Returning to Braque: "I never visualize a picture in my mind before starting to paint. On the contrary, I believe that a picture is finished only after one has completely effaced the idea that was there at the start."[5]

Poems can move *through* language into realms of experience not before encountered, and similarly can travel from experience into a pure and musical relationship with language. In either case, it's the motion I love and cherish.

And in fact, in 2004 astronomers discovered that there *is* a "sound" of the universe. Science fact: the universe is humming. A galaxy in the Perseus cluster approximately 250 million light years away is emitting a note: B-flat. Fifty-seven octaves below the piano's middle C.

1. Olga Broumas and T Begley, *Sappho's Gymnasium* (Port Townsend, WA: Copper Canyon Press, 1994), 161.

2. Susan Howe, *The Europe of Trusts* (Los Angeles: Sun and Moon Press, 1990), 36.

3. Ibid., 14.

4. Jean Valentine, *Door in the Mountain: New and Collected Poems* (Middletown, CT: Wesleyan University Press, 2004), 22.

5. Georges Braque, "In Painting There Must Be No Preconceived Idea," in *Painters on Painting,* ed. Eric Protter (Mineola, NY: Dover Publications, 1997), 210.

Yoko Ono's "Mulberry"

The Future Tense of History

Yoko Ono has written, "I think of my music more as a *gyo* (practice) than as a music."[1] In this sense, the music is *process* oriented, rather than *product* oriented. Each musical performance is a moment-in-time, a searching for personal revelation, rather than a recording to exist in "past-time," to be commodified and packaged for passive consumption.

When one thinks of music like this, issues of "like" or "dislike" or of aesthetic pleasure connected to experience are less relevant. Listening to it is a visceral, physical experience—because it is *real*—located in the body, because external concessions such as tunefulness, regular rhythm and time scheme are surrendered to the personal exploration of thematic geography of the voice.

"Mulberry" has several incarnations that move backwards in time and backwards from the point of "art" to the moment of art's origin. The first version was the most recent; it was a live recording of the song made in early 2001 and released on Ono's album *Blueprint for a Sunrise.* The earlier version of 1971 was a home recording made by Ono and John Lennon but not released until decades later as a bonus track on the CD re-release of *The Wedding Album.* The earliest version is the "original" version. It doesn't exist as a recording, only as the story of the origin of the song that Ono tells as a preface to the performance of the 2001 "Mulberry." In this way it is somewhat related to Ono's "Instruction Paintings," paintings created or realized according to a pre-written score. As one can only appreciate the art by both reading the instruction and looking at the painting, it is only by listening (actually and conceptually) to the three versions of "Mulberry" together that one can understand the many levels of meaning in this song.

At the beginning of the 2001 track, Ono tells the story of her life as a little girl with her brothers. The firebombing of Tokyo in 1943 destroyed whole districts of the downtown area—over 25 percent of the city had been incinerated, and thousands upon thousands of city dwellers fled the city to take refuge in the barns and outbuildings of farm families in the villages and towns around the capital. Ono relates what at first seems a simple childhood memory: she would go across the fields to the mulberry bushes to pick mulberries. Sometimes she would stay late, and the sun would begin to set, and she would run home across the field as the shadows lengthened. In her child's mind she imagined that ghosts—perhaps ghosts of Tokyo's dead—were chasing her across the fields to her home.

What kind of song might a child invent in order to capture a moment such as this? Should it be melodic? Should it conform to the twelve tones of the musical scale? Should it rhyme?

No one in the audience knows what might come next. A child's song for sure: the kind of tuneless, warbling singing that all children begin nearly at the same time they begin speech. Also with the same visceral and unashamed intensity that we will only allow ourselves as adults when we think we are alone at home or when we are in the shower in the morning. Ono sings, screams, wails, grunts and groans the single word "Mulberry" over the course of sixteen minutes, accompanied by Sean Ono Lennon's harsh guitar, imitating the gruesome, breathless noises of his mother's voice: a voice depicting the human suffering of that childhood moment carried across the years. A voice that accompanies not only the child's fears of those nights in the country, but back further to perhaps the song's secret seed—the firebombing of Tokyo itself.

The 1971 version of "Mulberry" is much different from the one that comes after it. It comes without the context of Yoko's public life. It moves us back in time—rather than adult son Sean, it's John, alive, warm, breathing again, who plays with Yoko, sometimes humming along, giving her verbal encouragement. The tragedies of her later life unpeel from her, and she sings to the young child in the countryside from a very different place. The later song is given from stage to a live audience; this "secret version" is sung only to John, in the privacy of their own apartment, a collaborative work for an audience of two.

But Ono's music is nothing if not generative. It returns over and over again to the seed of all of her art, her very first published work, an "instruction score" called "Secret Piece" which reads:

Decide on the one note you want to play. Play with the following accompaniment: the woods from 5am to 8am.[2]

At first it may seem nearly absurdly minimal, but this is the true power of Ono's art, and her music: that a single note of the human musician against the landscape of the world and history can teach you what history means, what art means, what music means: it is an individual spirit opening up her own powerful expressiveness against the harmonic backdrop of the whole universe.

When the flame that burns cities to ash falls from the sky in endless anger, what is left for the child running scared across the fields to do? Any words past the essential diminish the tragedy, the fear, that one moment. One word will have to do: "mulberry." And the way Ono tricks, teases, expands and expels that one word—of sustenance, of innocence and survival—is her "practice" of historical revelation through the only instrument that could possible "reveal" anything real: the individual human body.

NOTES

1. Yoko Ono, "To the Wesleyan People," in *YES Yoko Ono,* ed. John Hendricks and Alexandra Munroe (New York: Harry N. Abrams, 2000), 288.
2. Yoko Ono, "Secret Piece," in Hendricks and Munroe, *YES Yoko Ono,* 230.

How to Speak

Why write, if not in the name of an impossible speech?
—Michel de Certeau

Authentic speech is in trouble. The conceptual "voice" is troubled by generations of colonial interference and miseducation, and the actual physical speaking voice is traumatized by the inflections, sonic demands and syntactical sins of whole other language systems whose primary goal seems not the support of the human spirit but the support of a system of commercialism and global marketplaces that depend upon each other for survival. How can we speak honestly at all?

And can we speak in time? For, as the Western war on "terror," whether so-called or not, continues to affect the lives of millions of people around the world, questions of grammar become lethally relevant, as Terry Jones has pointed out: it is no more possible to win the war on "terror" than it is to win the war on "fear" or "murder" or "unhappiness."[1]

In *The Vertical Interrogation of Strangers,* Bhanu Kapil has fashioned a unique way to uncover the sounds of some of these occluded voices. She does so in a form that blurs the line between community and self, and de-centers the colonizer—if anything, she is engaged in an act of poetic decolonization.

The "strangers" in the title can as easily be the Indian women who were the focus of Kapil's ethnographic research as they could be all the strange women inside Kapil. The difference is blurred in the preface and is not cleared up in the following text. From the preface: "From January 12, 1992 to June 4, 1996 I traveled in India, England, and the United States, interviewing Indian women of diverse ages and backgrounds. Originally, my question to them was, 'Is it possible for you to say the thing you have never been able to say, not even to the one you have spent your whole life loving?'"[2]

The women, on the condition of anonymity, are given a space free of furniture, windows or overhead lighting in which to compose their answer. "My aim," writes Kapil, "was to ensure an honest and swift text, uncensored by guilt or the desire to construct an impressive, publishable 'finish.' In editing this anthology of responses I did not attempt to 'clean up' their roughness or rawness in terms of syntax, grammar, spelling, punctuation, or the way in which they filled the space of the page."

However, later in the introduction, Kapil confesses that she too answered the questions over and over again in her notebook. She wrote some responses on stickers that she left in public places ("escalator tubing, café tables, shop windows"), and others, it seems implied, may have ended up in the book. However, to what extent the book is an "anthology of responses," and to what extent it contains Kapil's own writings, she does not clarify. She merely says, "The voices of the women I met: pure sound. The shapes they made, as they moved through the world: methods. A way to describe my body. I didn't know where I was going."

The book itself then is a ward against dismemberment, a refutation of the postmodern idea that dismemberment is a new kind of wholeness. If it is true that to be dismembered is to be newly "whole" in a postmodern world, one wonders if that dismemberment is the same conceptually for people in the first world and people in the third or fourth world. Is the acceptance of dismemberment as a chronic condition an aesthetic gesture or a ward against metaphysical death, or is it a literal preparation for actual death? I only ask.

Following the preface is a page on which are listed the questions:

Twelve Questions

1. Who are you and whom do you love?
2. Where did you come from/how did you arrive?
3. How will you begin?
4. How will you live now?

5. What is the shape of your body?
6. Who was responsible for the suffering of your mother?
7. What do you remember about the earth?
8. What are the consequences of silence?
9. Tell me what you know about dismemberment.
10. Describe a morning you woke without fear.
11. How will you/have you prepare(d) for your death?
12. And what would you say if you could?[3]

The twelve listed questions progressed out of Kapil's original question: "Is it possible for you to say the one thing you have never been able to say, not even to the one you have spent your whole life loving?" To me it is completely terrifying to think that intimacy—*true* intimacy—is not possible. Likewise terrible to think—really think—that there are questions for which there is no answer. In a sense then this book is an exercise or investigation into the relationships between privacy and interiority and the possibilities of emotional intimacy if one leads an interior life.

Perhaps appropriately, it is not only Kapil who published responses to her questions; Jean Valentine has written a series of poems that answer various of Kapil's questions. Valentine also seems to know that the border between individuals is difficult to map: "Whatever kind of eyes you have now / lend to me—" she writes.

The book *Swoon,* by Nada Gordon and Gary Sullivan, comprised of the email transcripts of their long-distance correspondence, tells the story of how they were able to find intimacy across the distance of many miles—at the time Gordon lived in Tokyo and Sullivan in New York. Oddly or perhaps not so oddly, the two were able to create a great and passionate intensity that they were then unable to sustain at their first face-to-face meeting. The tension between an actual physical meeting and the concept of it is mirrored in the act of "publication," of making private or "secret" correspondence into literary commodities. As Kurt Cobain wrote inside the front cover of one of his many notebooks, "Please don't read this," and then just under that in the same handwriting—so presumably written at the same time—"Please read this while I am gone so you can figure me out." As Susan Howe writes it, "It is fun to be hidden, but horrible not to be found."[4]

Gordon and Sullivan *do* find each other, but confronted with an actual body rather than a literary representation of such, desire withers. Anne Carson has written about the key idea of eros—not the object itself, but the space, the lack, the distance between the object of love and the lover. The classical lover might write a letter to his love and have to wait—days, months; the unanswered letter quivers in the ether with the possibility of fulfillment.

How has our sense of the erotic changed with the instant gratification of email, of cell-phone communication? Unable to repair the damage to their intimacy by the actual physical meeting, Gordon and Sullivan resorted to writing notes to each other on a spiral notebook, sliding it back and forth across the table to one another to read and respond. "YOU CREATED ME," Sullivan writes, "BUT I ALREADY EXIST." Gordon responds a little later, "(then what's going with me? what's my problem?)" and "(why parentheses?) / (how do I really feel?)"[5]

Is it easier to be intimate in writing because there is no risk? Has the very act of physical touch become compromised? It is that intimacy of touch that has no place in either publication or the public sphere. We even have a phrase against this particular behavior: "public displays of affection."

There in the bar, face-to-face, Gordon and Sullivan were not privately musing or writing, but speaking *to* someone. The space between letters that Carson talks about still exists, but the transference carries with it the possibility of *immediacy*—there is no chance really to "take something back." Communication is irretrievable and direct—for the most part, letters cannot go astray. A letter writer has no recourse—his work is attached to him. One cannot duck away from responsibility—emotional or otherwise—for what one says. In a sense, even intimate communication is subjected to the same codes of understanding that once only governed "publication."

In a way, "publication" could now be taken to mean any kind of making public of one's own mind—even if only to one other, even if only to "the one you have spent your whole life loving." What can we make now of Dickinson's "Publication—is the

Auction / Of the Mind of Man"? It is distressing to think that even to speak—to speak of ideas at all—is to reduce the "Human Spirit / To Disgrace of Price."[6]

We similarly do not know which of the answers contained in Kapil's book are her own original responses and which are the responses yielded by her anthropological surveys—or whether those surveys were only metaphorical and not literal, referring only to Kapil's own process of self-excavation. It's easy enough to ask the author, but less interesting. It is better to be in the dark about what the nature of this book is, about who is speaking. This ambiguity of speaking voices somehow enables, the way fumbling in the dark for a lover might, a greater and more immediate intimacy, without the complications of awareness, between reader and writer.

Amidst the progression of questions, the answers come from clearly different women, with different languages and different geographies. Each speaks earnestly, seriously, and once in a brief while what seems to be a more autobiographically immediate voice appears. Out of the lyric plucks, an emotional narrative begins to uncover itself: "Sometimes, for days, weeks even, she forgets that she is going to die."[7] Each of the women-voices speaks out of a need to experience, define and divine—the writer herself, at some undisclosed point, begins an interaction with them. That boundary, like the "long dark border between India and Pakistan," mentioned in the text, remains unmapped.[8]

If troubling, it seems a reflection of our real lives: bombarded as we are with the constant language of commercialism and consumption—the language of scripts of movies and television programs, learning at younger ages the communication patterns, speech patterns and rhetorical devices of unreal, soulless beings, to the extent that our interactions with one another, from the very public to the very intimate, assume the sick and unfunny aura of ventriloquism. Sick and unfunny because the new "authentic" voice is not corporeal but corporate.

Melissa Wolsak, in *An Heuristic Prolusion,* writes, "Writing is my way of listening and ventriloquising until I reach the place of speaking."[9] If "speaking" (even if it is a form of writing) is the form of utterance that's closest to us—closest to intimacy and authenticity—then it is a powerful thing to "practice" "writing

and listening" as a way of getting to that point of authentic utterance, which in the unmapped borders between Kapil and her
strangers remains unknown.

If questions have answers, they are lost in the noise of our
lives. "What is a question?" asks Kapil in her essay on Valentine's
poems. "Literally, it's a way of gathering information but not of
processing it. As a mode of enquiry that's also, linguistically,
founded on doubt, on not having the words for what passed between you and another person at the end of a relationship, the
question seals space."[10]

The oracles at Delphi spoke in discontinuous couplets. It is
not possible for the truth to be "revealed" at all, but it can only
be told in a puzzle. An oracle adventuring to speak the truth
could become "ecstatic" in the classical sense: she loses her
senses, moves outside herself. It is an interesting distinction from
the idea of becoming "intimate": that it is only possible once you
leave the limitations of your own sensual perceptions. So we can
only "know" Kapil once she is no longer corporeal and assumes
into herself the voices of the multitude of strangers. But you
never know where you've gotten until you get there. It is risky to
try to know oneself. Kapil writes: "You want to live? Finally, you're
alone. The ice drifts in the hollows. You walked here. The sheer
maroon cliffs. The silver bones of your pelvis. The bright blue
sky. Your bloodstone. This water. Something huge and without
music has just happened."[11]

In her book, questions begin to fold into themselves. They
appear in the answers to other questions, or the answers wander
far away from the original question. One issue the book presses
against is this: the English language enacts colonization: there is
a Subject which Acts-Upon an Object. The pattern of question
and answer enacts the same motion—a questioner who delin-
eates the area of engagement, the answerer who endeavors to
construct a linguistic response that adheres to the main prin-
ciples articulated. But more frequently, Kapil's voices swerve
away from such a system of binaries—more frequently engaging
in dialectic response, answering the same questions over and
over again, and in radically different ways, or more disturbingly,
refusing to answer the questions at all.

Sometimes, like with the Delphic oracle, eerie truth is voiced in the answer that swerves: "TELL ME WHAT YOU KNOW ABOUT DISMEMBERMENT: 'His coat was made of rain, and the torn-off covers of English paperbacks, and human hair. It smelled of the earth, then; the twin histories of nostalgia, and bonesnapping.'" To remember the past in a nostalgic air becomes a version of dismemberment. "The distances between my body and the bodies of the ones I love: grow," writes Kapil. "I have a few questions to ask, but I do not know how to break the growing silence."

Kapil's book, though, moves beyond the simpler question of an individual's move to "publication," into the area of social context for expression. Inherent in the questions and their answers is the problem of a self, constrained from speaking by a complex set of social systems and a governing world, many times, for Indian women, personified at the family level. Ultimately what emerges from the kaleidoscopic call-and-response format is a kind of answer—if as fragmented and "dismembered" as other "postmodern" writing, it is more descriptive of the social reality of women seeking true expression; less an artistic or aesthetic decision.

But Wolsak writes, "For me the urgent question is . . . 'do we have a prayer?'" By prayer she means a deliverance from current conditions of suffering. Of course it is naïve to think now that single prayers are going to be able to undo a global system that depends on both the exploitation of labor and natural resources and the suppression of creative thought and authentic expression to further itself, but it is worth considering what a "prayer" is linguistically: exactly what I have been talking about—an authentically true expression of inner desire, directed at an entity able to fulfill those desires, and—like Gordon and Sullivan's emails to one another—an expression directly given and directly received.

Any prayer—written or spoken—is the opposite of an author's dismemberment—it is an assertion of the body as a field of non-physical energy actualized within a physically present body in the world. And so perhaps all prayers are secret. Ultimately, Kapil's respondents begin to distrust the questioner: "I don't know how this corresponds to the world," writes one. In order to preserve authenticity, the answerer is given her own room, encouraged to speak for as long as she likes and of whatever she likes. The prayer is in the unplanned utterance. "Somebody is asking me the question. I reply, 'Coffee, please,' and the moonlight turns into pure red sun, and then the clouds, and then the earth."[12]

These women and women-within who speak do so in a constructed environment: the room without windows, overhead lighting furniture, etc. The acts they describe and write of engage the events of their lives in a context without consequence. In an extreme and powerful moment, answering the question "TELL ME WHAT YOU KNOW ABOUT DISMEMBERMENT," one woman describes going to the Tate Gallery to look at the painting *The Lady of Shallot*.[13] In the painting, the Lady of Shallot is in her boat, transfixed, depicted by the painter at the moment the curse has come upon her. While the museum guard looks distractedly at his hands, the woman leans forward and slices out a piece of the painting—the candle flames. As if the "meaning" is talismanic and part of the actual fabric of the cloth, the woman attempts to enact her own "re-memberment" by taking a piece of collective discourse, i.e., a painting hanging in a gallery, "stealing" it back, taking it home with her.

If dismemberment is a preparation for death, which intimacy requires, then shouldn't we consciously seek that dismemberment? And if we were to say it is all conceptual rather than actual, how is this line of thinking different from a very Christian-martyrdom view of the world—the view that got us into so much trouble in the first place? Is it a form of dismemberment itself, a form of suppressing speech, to not write about the real world, to write about art and ideas? No: it is radically essential to begin promoting the process of thoughtfulness and engaged living. As the prophet Mohammad famously declared, "One hour of study is worth sixty years of worship." How close was sixty years to the average life span of the time? I think it is possible then that the prophet meant that study was worth one's entire life.

"I can't even begin," one of Kapil's strangers writes, and then several pages later, "I want to begin."

Sullivan and Gordon continue to "begin"—to find ways of bringing public language and private expression into concert;

they go on to become primary figures in the Flarf poetry movement, a movement which attempts the use of public language in order to find some level of private communication, a political attempt perhaps at putting the language of capital in service of the human individual. Its success remains to be seen. For Valentine, at any rate, the route to the authentic voice is internal and does not need to be proven: "with you it wasn't flesh and blood, it was under: / I know you brokenheart before this world, / and I know you after."[14]

It is interesting that Sullivan closes the main narrative of *Swoon* not with a private email to Gordon, but with a post to a listserv: a poem about her that ends, "I'll close now having in your absence only everything still to stay."[15] There is both postscript (poems by Sullivan and Gordon to one another written from their now shared space in Brooklyn) and afterword (a prose note by Chris Stroffolino), but to me it feels better to leave the possibility of authentic utterance with Gordon's "absence" as a generative force. Intimacy doesn't require actual death; it is the notion of not dying that makes it so sweetly possible.

Kapil's last stranger writes, "I do not think I will die today." So we have a prayer.

NOTES

1. Terry Jones, "Why Grammar Is the First Casualty of War," *London Daily Telegraph,* January 12, 2002.

2. Bhanu Kapil Rider, *The Vertical Interrogation of Strangers* (Berkeley: Kelsey St. Press, 2001), 6.

3. Ibid., 9.

4. Susan Howe, *The Midnight* (New York: New Directions Books, 2003), 127.

5. Nada Gordon and Gary Sullivan, *Swoon* (New York: Granary Books, 2001), 167–69.

6. Emily Dickinson, "Publication—is the Auction / Of the Mind of Man," in *The Poems of Emily Dickinson,* ed. R. W. Franklin (Cambridge: Harvard University Press, 1998), 742.

7. Bhanu Kapil Rider, *The Vertical Interrogation of Strangers* (Berkeley: Kelsey St. Press, 2001), 22.

8. Ibid., 13.

9. Melissa Wolsak, *An Heuristic Prolusion* (Vancouver: Friends of Runcible Mountain, 2000).

10. Bhanu Kapil, "The Unwelt Question," unpublished manuscript.

11. Rider, *The Vertical Interrogation of Strangers,* 25.

12. Ibid., 43.

13. Ibid., 44.

14. Jean Valentine, *Little Boat* (Middletown, CT: Wesleyan University Press, 2007), 57.

15. Gordon and Sullivan, *Swoon,* 299.

2

Poetry and Painting

On a cloudy day, at the ocean, staring out at the horizon, one can see two things. That the earth does curve. And that the place at which the sky and the sea meet disappears.

In the fall of 1999 I moved to New York City with a backpack full of clothes, a blank journal and a couple of books. In one of them, *Ink Dark Moon,* Jane Hirshfield's translations of Izumi Shikibu and Ono no Komachi, I had been writing little response poems underneath the text.

I felt like I had been emptying myself in preparation for this huge life change—a different city, going back to school after four years in the workforce, leaving behind people that I loved, arriving somewhere new, frightened, listless, alone.

It had all the weight of pilgrimage—we go to haunted places, sacred places, places of immense natural beauty—the desert, the ocean, the mountains—we go there, starving and ready to eat.

Before I went back to school to study poetry, I painted. I had no education in it, but during my years of working in the public policy and organizing arenas, I found the need for a kinetic art. And it was indeed kinetic for me. The surface of a painting can be in motion or approximate motion, and there is a relationship between the painter's body and the canvas too that is a physical and fraught space.

The poet wishes to be so arduously involved in tubes of color, brushes, the grain of canvas—what happens to a painting when a layer of acrylic is left long enough and then disturbed with new color and shapes. A poet doesn't know it, but he is also dealing with same gift—there is no erasure; early drafts and versions haunt writing, suffuse it. Always the earlier poem hovers like a ghost at the edges of the writer's mind. He's a lucky one who can coax it back into the field of actuality.

Perhaps this is why I, as a painter, always chose to work with acrylics rather than oils or any other finer kinds of paint. As a painter, there's no idea of revision. I'm rather adding layers on top of layers. Acrylic holds its shape but still resists the new strokes. Impossible texture is achieved by placing a dark color against light. Shading and internal glow come through with a wet rag taken to strokes not yet dried—the *material* itself allows the "revision" process to blend (seamlessly or not, as you like) with the original generative process.

What's on the page may be a written trace, but the poem as a conceptual moment in time or an action in space still reacts against new revision.

Though I had painted and had ideas about painting, I had never truly been an art lover—never had truly *seen* and been fed by paintings. That October I went to the Metropolitan Museum of Art and saw paintings that changed my understanding of poetry.

On the first floor, in the Egyptian Wing, I saw work by the contemporary Egyptian artist Farouk Hosny. So frequently museum showings of art of non-Western cultures are relegated to the safely ancient and exotic, or to the paintings that are directly influenced by European idioms and forms. Hosny is nothing like this.

His landscapes are pointedly abstract but rooted in an Egyptian vocabulary of color, form and movement. The canvases are huge, and layered. The history of them can be seen, faded and alarmed, iconic symbols littered at the edges and lyrical shapes— an arching crescent, stars, triangular shapes—floating among the washes of color.

In Egyptian art, once decolonization occurred at the beginning of the twentieth century and the Egyptian people, free from foreign rule after millennia—Greeks, Romans, Arabs, Turks, French, English—began to work in modern art forms, an amazing thing happened: what were subsequent periods of Western modern art—classicism, neo-classicism, impressionism, modernism, abstract expressionism, postmodernism—happened immediately and simultaneously.

When the great temple of Abu Simbel was deconstructed and reconstructed on higher ground, threatened by flooding caused by the building of the modern-day temple, the Aswan High Dam, the destroyed statue—second from the left—was reconstructed in its destroyed state. Why wouldn't it be?

In a dance, parts of the choreographic process are *rehearsed* away. In less interesting paintings, the work is pronounced solid and finished—no stray marks exist to show it was once made. Similarly, in staged performance arts, we are meant *not* to see the efforts of the actors.

I am so interested, for this reason, in the sculptures of Camille Claudel—later Rodin and Zadkine both copy her. In Claudel's work, the sculptures begin to emerge from the larger piece of rock from which they were carved. At some critical point of non-completion, she *abandons* the sculpture. No, not abandons—rather, Claudel allows the sculpture to exist at the moment *between*. Eve *made*, Eve-*as*-Rib, perhaps even *still within* the Body of Adam.

Why should art complete itself? Ought not the artist surrender at least part of it?

I climbed to the second floor, and in the Modern Art Wing, I caught my first glimpse of Hans Hofmann. Ten of his paintings from the last two years of his life—*The Renate Series*—were being exhibited side by side. What do I love the most about Hofmann? Is it the profusion of color? The intense dedication to physicality that both the shapes depicted and the surface of the canvas itself represent? I think it is the dynamic and dramatic tension he brought to the canvas by repudiating classical laws of perspective. It is impossible to tell which is the foreground and which is the background in a Hofmann painting. Whether one is figure or landscape, it becomes irrelevant.

How could a poet not love this? Walter Pater must have been dreaming about Hofmann in 1873 when he wrote, "All art aspires to the condition of music."

It's poetry that Hofmann was dreaming about when he painted, as evidenced by his lovely and lyrical titles: *Profound Longing, Deep Within the Ravine, Renate's Nantucket, To Miz: Pax Vobiscum.*

Full of Hofmann, I went on a trip to France in the summer of 2000, and while I traveled—several weeks in Paris, and then by train through Provence with stints in Cassis and Arles, before heading to Corti in the heart of Corsica, where I lost myself beautifully—I encountered art without the language to describe it.

Surrounded by people I loved, speaking a language I didn't know, my poems pared themselves down from pages and pages into six or seven lines each. It was amazing being separated from my vocabulary. I found myself using only those English words I could approximate in French. All the spaces that existed in my conversation due to my lack of knowledge replicated themselves in the poems I was writing.

Only there, in that moment of loss and gain, could I have seen the paintings of Nicolas de Staël and known them. I watched as de Staël's abstract earlier works slowly returned to the space of realism, and with his images—seagulls, a train, a tree, a boat, all began to emerge from the pulsing color fields—I learned what Hofmann's dynamic perspective applied to poetry might sound like. I learned also how to look at Hofmann again, to understand finally that Rothko's work was *not* minimalism, that my current experience of linguistic lack could approximate that traveling experience better than I could hope to do in my journals—which unlike the poems I was writing were full of properly ordered sentences and paragraphs.

Do we merely dissolve into each other? Is there no figure or landscape, only the field of shapes and colors? De Staël returned me to the world of objects.

When I returned to the States that fall, I immediately went back to the museum. Though the Hofmann show had long since closed, I first saw the work of Agnes Martin.

What can I say here when silence would be most accurate?

I haven't been silent about it in fact—two poems about my experience looking at Agnes Martin paintings appear in *The Far Mosque*. In one I tried to interrogate philosophically the ideas of the paintings; in the other I tried to use language mimetically to demonstrate what it was *like* to look at one.

Still, it is always a question of form and how one forms poems. How does previous experience inform the final shape of the poem—I mean in the lines and phrases? How can one choose *not* to revise out the errors, the missteps, the stuttering, the stray marks and confusions?

Agnes Martin wrote once, "You wouldn't think of form at the ocean."

Her canvases are both formal and formless, blank and governed by the grids she drew across them in graphite pencil. One is tempted to think of her as a minimalist, or even—as Martin thought of herself—as a classicist interested in form and design. But the canvases themselves belie it. Martin worked purely by hand—the squares are irregular, the lines not mathematically straight—the human element, the lovely emotion of it, governs these cool works. Their titles, like Hofmann's, progress from the minimal (*untitled*) to the suggestive (*The Beach, The Harvest*) to the shamelessly sentimental (*Innocence, Lovely Life, Everyday Happiness*).

But it was the carefully worked surface that really broke my heart. What appears to be blankness or whiteness from ten feet away dissolves into an amazing, worked texture on close examination. The painting I saw at the Met that first day was drawn, pointed, littered with marks—brilliantly alive. Somewhere I read that Martin could spend a year on a single canvas. You can tell when you see traces of submerged shapes under cool washes of white or gray. Somewhere else I remember reading that she once stopped painting for nearly a decade.

Martin also saw art as a process, writing, "I imagine my paintings as beach you must cross to get to the ocean."

What is that ocean? What is that place where the sea and sky evaporate or condense? Why write poems or make paintings in a dangerous world? For Martin it was simple: "Beauty and happiness and life are all the same and they are pervasive, unattached and abstract and they are our only concern. They are immeasurable, completely lacking in substance. They are perfect and sublime. This is the subject matter of art."

Radha Says

Considering the Last Poems of Reetika Vazirani

Breath moves through a poetic line beginning to end, but in Reetika Vazirani's three volumes of poetry we see a different treatment of breath—breath that interrupts itself, sometimes in mid-exhale, breath that swirls around and returns, as it does at the top of an inhale or the bottom of an exhale in the yogic practice of *pranayama.* "Yoga is a discipline of tenderness for and awareness of the body," Vazirani writes in her essay "The Art of Breathing," "heart, lungs, kidney, pressure points to the inner life of the eye, third eye, eye of the spleen." It's this motion of bodily compassion and this belief in the quiet micromovements of lyric moments within an otherwise narrative poem that distinguish Vazirani's work as it has evolved through her first two published collections. The range of her accomplishment can now be seen with the publication of *Radha Says.*

Throughout her first two books of poetry, *White Elephants* and *World Hotel,* Reetika Vazirani sought ways of bringing the rhythms and poetic structures of Indian languages, forms of poetry and concepts of the poetic line into English. As in the work of Meena Alexander and Agha Shahid Ali, Vazirani's English sometimes retains a sense of the foreign as a result. In all three writers, the primary harvest of this hybridity is music and emotional intensity, but a subtle sense also enters of the very real dangers involved in being a body "between"—between cultures, between languages, between nations.

Like Ali, Vazirani, in the space of disruption, finds her answer in form. In the space of her breath and body, like Alexander, she finds the answer in peculiarly torqued language, a mixing of dictions, a juxtaposition of images of sublimity and violence. Like ancient Hindu temple art, Vazirani's bawdiness and her body-ness are always in service of a search for transcendence, spiritual weight and physical material desire two sides of the same coin. She draws the best of Ali's love for the form of a line and a poem and Alexander's desire to ratchet up emotional tension, and braids these together into her own unique approaches.

It's essential to understand that her attention to form is an attention to the way the line works on its own and as a hinge between what comes before and after. Because of this the poems are nearly impossible to excerpt. In "Mahadevi to Kaushik," she writes:

> . . . at dusk you walked me to the red dome
> you went for my hips when I offered you a rose
> morning the white stone blinded me
> you split   a tiger from blooms
> useless why did you frisk me
> send your drummers out   unzip other limbs

The lines can be heard three ways, each as an answer to the line before it, on its own as a line in the present moment of lust and then of course as the beginning of an enjambed thought continuing with the following line and perhaps (or perhaps not) also with the line after that. It's a common construction in the poems that follow—lines that turn and churn, sometimes referring to what came before, sometimes leading to the line after and sometimes just floating on the surface of the moment, there, themselves. Also, the heady event described here floats in time, one line at dusk, two lines later in the morning. Vazirani's quirky lack of punctuation, particularly commas, allows us to experience the lines more directly in body and breath: stranger, sexier.

Unlike Ali and Alexander, whose various attentions to a poem's formal qualities seem concerned with trying to weave together disparate experiences, in Vazirani's lines, there is always a sprawling laxity that flirts with the opposite impulse, to dissipate, disperse, fall apart. Here is the opening of "They Loved Ruin" in the book's final section:

> . . . wonderful to have lost you
> domicile   the life   gigantic
> hotel   when I speak to you
> I speak of myself   apple in a worm's day
> star   parched   this hole-in-one feeling

Notice how the line breaks and the mid-line caesuras work together to carry energy of thought and emotion through the poem beginning to end. Vazirani's caesuras likewise do not always have typographical spaces delineating them (as in the line "useless why did you frisk me," quoted above).

In the Ghalib poems of the second section, there is a charming narrative voice and a charmingly unfractured recounting of experiences. These prose poems play with the expected unity of a narrative primarily by voice of the speaker rather than by narrative or dramatic device. For example, in the first paragraph of "Ghalib's Prophecy of His Death, 1860–1861," the poet tells about his cousin's visit from Delhi, deriding the poet for his conviction. In the second paragraph, the poet endeavors to convince his cousin of his seriousness, but in the third paragraph the cousin departs, vowing not to return again for twenty years. One is left to read between the lines, or in this case, between the paragraphs, to understand the lingering sense of loss and alienation.

Like the Ghalib poems, many of the poems in the following section are written in persona, but in this case, as opposed to the mythological poems of the opening section, there is a conflation between a contemporary speaker and the mythical figure of Radha, in legend Krishna's consort. Though Vazirani writes in fairly short lines, the suspension of lines as full units, combined with unexpected enjambments and the nearly complete lack of punctuation, functions to force the reader to swim in a lake of sound and words, with a sense of breath as liquid that will enter all the openings of silence to fill them:

> Diana says beat your song
> from this yellow Vrindavan horizon
> speak to yourself as you would speak to God
> no not to Krishna whose eyes stirred in you
> the costume-loving bride   what comes
> of fame but banquet gazes

Indeed, in addition to lines which feed into each other, sometimes there is a literal conflation of identity. "Maya Sita Rita Radha I've been," Vazirani writes in "Radha on Queen Maya in Red Sandstone." Objects move into and out of the body. In "Art of Breathing" Vazirani describes breath in her own body: "The heat in my body leads me to spaces within myself, as if to rooms in a house I had never let myself fully inhabit. I can enter deep and secret rooms, light and dark rooms—spaces between my vertebrae and the warm pouch of my pancreas." In these lines from the poem "Seeta" in *World Hotel,* one can feel the syntax and line breaks shifting across sentences and musical units to create in the reader some of that breath music that only a regular practitioner of *pranayama* could compose:

> I was the orphan Seeta. And the mother of.
> That is over. I am tired.
> I think, sunshine on ships
> when I traveled, laughs on Malabar Hill—
> my life did not comprise me it was so brief.

When a reader must shift across a line to construct meaning, as in the first line of the excerpt, or disrupt grammatical expectation, as in the last line with its missing period, he becomes an active participant in the poem's music. There is a transference between reader and writer, between written text and pronounced text, between the external and internal, between both sides of the breath. In this passage from "From Patanjali," Vazirani seems to be reflecting on the way things from the outside world and the inside world (the body) join each other:

> or else the heart-memory half of me
> the way almonds taste on first tongue
> I open my fingers and feel their breath
> or else centuries pouring into out of
> people yes we judge them light and dark

Later in this masterful poem, she reflects on the bodily connection with her son:

                        you
        son   deep sleep dreamless
        my own skin   I am in
        you   in your rest

Throughout the manuscript there is a sense of joining—with
vastness and small individuality, with mortality and eternity, with
expanse and locality. It all happens in the context of smallness,
though—individual bodies, individual lives—though throughout there is also a denial of limitation. "I was raised either/or,"
the speaker of "Beyond Honey Soul Body and Rose" confesses,
but later decides, "I am counting down / instead of up the scale
to Allah." In another poem, the speaker observes:

        I drop my watch in a tin bucket   the sun
        never creeps till I am done with him

In this dizzying and attentive music, everything seems at stake.
In the blistering and revealing poem "She Knows Krishna Will
Leave," the poet writes, "I savor the jilted / havoc of my breath."
But these poems, this breath, is anything but havoc. One is des-
perate to believe, after all, that every human life, whatever its
gifts or crimes, sought to see.

    In the rough draft of her title poem "Radha Says," Vazirani in-
vokes Ruth Stone, Lucille Clifton and Hayden Carruth by name.[1]
We look to poetry to build for ourselves a community to carry us
through the moments of our lives; perhaps Vazirani was also
participating in the yogic practice of naming one's gurus or influences. Reetika Vazirani has given us a valuable and troubling
document, visceral, powerful, immense and deeply felt. Whatever else she was, Reetika Vazirani wrote these poems down, this
"round robin collage," to say a little bit about "how skin learned
to hold the given bones."

    "For," she sang, "if you speak honestly / to yourself perhaps
one morning / you will speak to God."

                            NOTE

    1. Stone and Clifton are mentioned only by last name. The draft is
more fully cited in the editors' afterword to the collection.

Little Map
A Valentine

In Islamic architecture, the interior of a mosque is strangely empty. The shapes of the exterior are round, inviting—the arch, the dome—but otherwise, just an expanse of floor, an interior without structure. The experience of the desert, for both artists and pilgrims, is similarly one of removing external contexts; the singularity of sand and sky—like the mountains, or the ocean, other sites of pilgrimage—removes fluctuations of thought and dares one to focus.

Similarly, in the poems of Jean Valentine, there always seems to be a narrative, a real situation of emotion, but it is told in outlines, seen in the dark. In "October Morning," she writes:

> October morning—
> sea lions barking
> on the off-shore rock
>
> Autumn evening—
> seals' heads nosing through the
> the pink Pacific
>
> I gather myself
> onto my day raft, your voice
> lost under me:
> first other tongue.[1]

It's easy to say you get lost in Jean Valentine's poems, but you don't. You get found. Each stanza here places you in time and space, allowing the physical description that follows to be anchored. If she "turns," she swerves not into the unknown, which for her is always a linguistic space, but into a real and concrete lived space where it seems to matter less whether linguistic structures assert themselves or, as they occasionally do, disappear.

Here, she gathers herself on the abstract "day raft," but by leaving the first half of the phrase "your voice lost under me" on the same line, she implies that the raft is the voice of the other. She finishes with an otherwise awkward construction that here functions sonically: "first other tongue."

In tarot cards, the last card of the major arcana, and also the first—the culmination of the journey and the beginning of the next journey, a card without a number—is "The Fool." It is best to come to Valentine's poems a little dumb, a little empty-headed. In the "House and the World," she begs for some release:

> All this anger
> heart beating
>
> unless I'd come inside
> your blind window
> and stay there like you[2]

She knows though there is more than the blindness, the insideness, of the angry one. She wants

> the cello part
> carrying us the whole time

and all the other strange experiences the poem promises are yet to come: the "tipped groin," the "flying whitehorn hedge," the "cup."

Many poems that traffic in disruption, new syntactic systems, perhaps in the heat of the erotic moment might lose the nouns at the beginning of sentences, or contain sentences that could dissolve, but in Valentine's poems, the fragments are not meant either to mourn the lost whole, nor to function as a small collage bit—a new form of postmodern veracity. Think of them rather as a jigsaw, perhaps a jigsaw with a few missing pieces, maybe a lot of missing pieces. Valentine is a writer of poems of personal experience the way Jane Cooper was, the way Eleanor Ross Taylor is. In this sense, though she is revolutionary in terms of craft and technique, she is nearly "old school," by which I mean "confessional."

In her earliest work, her rhythms unfolded as long phrases, usually repeating themselves, imitating the lulling sound of the waves, or a mother's voice, or the individual consciousness drifting into sleep. In her poem "September 1963," she writes, "Tears stay with me, stay with me tears. / Dearest, go: this is what / School is, what the world is." And by the end of the poem, she eschews epiphany and goes for the drifting:

> Glad, derelict, I find a park bench, read
> Birmingham, Birmingham, Birmingham.
> White tears on a white ground,
> White world going on, white hand in hand,
> World without end.[3]

Claudia Rankine wrote, "The languaged self, then, in order to keep itself human, in order to cohere, has to fragment. The '*I.*' exists in time and is married to biological, personal, historical, and cultural meaning. Not to realize this is to commit a blink of omission." Valentine's speakers have the same porous identity. They are real, they are her, to be sure, but also they are us, they exist in the world of commonality and universality. Rankine notes further that we cannot do with the totally hermetic or symbolic in art: "The 'I' ultimately has a responsibility to the 'you.' It recognizes we are always being broken into by history."

The idea of "autobiography" in Valentine's work is the introduction of alchemy: the secret experiment which preserves the individual experience against the grid of the poem. In her poem "The Pen," she asks:

> who taught me to know instead of not to know?
> And this pen   its thought
>
> Lying on the thought of the table
> A bow lying across the strings
>
> Not moving
> Held[4]

The pen, thought of, but by misplaced possessive, belongs to the thought-of itself—language devouring itself, the object and thought, too—Plato undone by Valentine.

Who is lying on the thought of the table: the pen or its thought? Or is "thought" used the way it is in the previous line, as in: that which the *table* thought—

Or perhaps: "A bow lying across the strings" is lying on the thought of the table.

And if *lying* instead implies prevaricating?

I trust, always, to be brought to the moment of music. This music—the music vibrating through the body of the poem upon its completion—the music of strange dreams and wise totem animals—though it could be also that music of absolute potential energy: the moment the violinist lays her bow on the strings but has not yet begun to play.

In "Child," Valentine writes:

> you are in a blind
> desert   child
>
> your "too-muchness" is written
> in the Torah
>
> child   it is written
> in the pit
>
> written in the black fire
> on white fire
>
> deer star
> black star
>
> third star
> who sees[5]

Each line exists singly here. In bare observation of Valentine's words whipping by and disappearing into the wind, it seems the individual line, and not the phrase or sentence, is the unit she is placing her words into—like Sappho, whose fragments assemble tantalizingly close to a picture, her poems seem to hover at the edge of "closure" but make adamant refusal of arrival. Yet these poems are filled not with intangible concepts, but with simpler things: a pitcher, a pen, a blue dictionary propping a window open.

There *is* an embracing of the notion of emotional truth to be adduced from poetry, but there is a definite rejection of the poet as guide of the reader to that place, as if one is being led by the hand halfway into the forest and then left there.

Yet the child in the desert is blind. The desert is blind. The three stars know there is a space language can't go.

The writing of the poem degrades from positions of authority (the "Torah") *through* positions of lack of material authority, but perhaps a very deeply personal authority ("the pit"), and into the alchemical place—a place governed by nature and its chaotic processes, beyond the ego of the personal and beyond the "separate" life of the personal—the white fire. The black fire.

The "final" space entered is a space in which the primary emblems of our mythologies—the stars one might follow in the desert expecting to arrive eventually—and why not?—at a child—are revealed not as emblems for an external myth, nor as shamanistic amulets for the internal myths, but as something of a conflation of the two. As Hans Hofmann has written, "Art is magic. So say the surrealists. But how is it magic? In its metaphysical development? Or does some final transformation culminate in a magical reality? In truth the latter is impossible without the former." To read Valentine is to find oneself in the layered drama of her poems, but safely held in a recognizable world. You think you don't have a map, but your own life is your map.

In "Little Map," she writes:

> The white pine
>
> The deer coming closer
>
> The ant
> In my bowl
> —where did she go
> when I brushed her out?
>
> The candle
> —where does it go?

                    Our brush with each other
                    —two animal souls
                    without cave
                    image
                    or
                    word[6]

When Valentine travels outside the language—into an instinc-
tual region—*where* can she be said to have gone? Plato may ask
us to accept that there is a cave, that there are those who are ca-
pable of leaving it and experiencing the true light, but neither
he nor anyone after can ever offer anything other than a sub-
jective confirmation of what's always known:

In the beginning of the map, we are given the most primitive
of maps: individual, localized images—ones which do not immediately have a referent; as in the question of Hofmann's backgrounds, the lines drawn between the deer, the pine, the ant,
are dependent on the viewers' experience—the "fragments" are
given as whole phrases, and without the *incomplete* quality of the
fragment.

The *ruin* becomes a *rune.*

In the earlier poem "Silences: A Dream of Governments,"
Valentine explores further a fragmenting of experience:

                    Then
              the plain astonishment—the air
              broken open: just ourselves
              sitting, talking; like always;
              the kitchen window
              propped open by the same
              blue-gray dictionary.
              August.   Rain.   A Tuesday.

              Then, absence.[7]

It's the absence that makes the mosque. Inside, unlike in the
church, there are rarely pillars, rarely rows of chairs, no altar—
rather, alcove, galleries, prayer niche; space for bodies, for
smoke, for intention—

There's something of space for intention, as well as Hofmann's interest in spatially de-centering "context," in Valentine's line "August. Rain. A Tuesday." It is the image given through the word—the deer, the pine; the lizard, the road; the dictionary, the window; the moment when the word struggles between the "word" ("representation of") and the "of" (can there even *be* a "subject"?) that creates the wish in me that writing could be as "plastic" as canvas and paints in contemporary abstract color-field painting.

In these paintings, one needs no referent "comprehension." Syntax neither determines nor undermines the meaning. The painting's language liberated from "form" (though, as Georges Braque notes, all language gives "form" to silence) casts out into "unknowable." The painting, however, at least has a "picture-plane," bordered by frame and existent in dimensional space. The canvas gives a literal "stanza" to move around in.

Within that "stanza" phrases can be articulated, re-articulated, appear and disappear—as they frequently do.

The most stunning of arts are not those which fix together seamlessly, but those radioactive ones, those with dangerous half-lives, those which degrade just before our eyes.

As always, the space *between* is the story.

Valentine uses a statement by Joseph Bruchac as the epigraph of her book *Growing Darkness, Growing Light:* "I . . . like to deal with the relationship between growing darkness and growing light, the dusk and the dawn, those times when there is a chance to see transition. . . . The dream is a connection, another transitional time. . . . In dreams we sometimes can see resemblances of where we really came from, whether we can explain it or not."[8] There is something of Nadezhda Mandelstam in the work that Valentine does, though rather than walking around for years with the poems of someone else living in her memory, Valentine, one gets the sense, is remembering her own over the course of a long time when everything extra spills out and we are left with the richest distillation.

Where does the candle go—

Valentine will come to the real world and say—why then go into lands of dreams, half lands? It isn't that these poems occupy the place of *half-light* in the space between the "dream" world and the living world, or in the moment of "the luminous room," rather that these places—"daylight," "luminous room," "dream-state"—are all tropes for a living "reality."

. . . deer star black star third star who sees—

Her work turns on the thought, not on the word. It is this essential notion—the act of restoring past experience to present immediacy, to "this world"—that makes reading a Jean Valentine poem such an active experience. And since her poems turn so much on the thought, the rhythm of that thought becomes the rhythm of language. Fraught and freighted with silences, Valentine's poems are a sonic pleasure. "Fears: Night Cabin" begins with short, truncated images:

> Snake   tick
> black widow
> brown recluse

The brief overture is followed by three separate images, each perhaps representing one of the "fears" of the title. Each image has a separate lineation; each has separate rhythm of language:

> —The truck last night on 79
> dragging a chain
>
> —A Cloud
> rounding slowly
> at the window
>
> —The wick   unlit
> curled cold in the kerosene lamp.[9]

The first line of the final couplet echoes the sounds of the opening, while the second, with its opening hard consonants, gives way quickly, with the word "kerosene," to the closing image.

With the most delicate of images—for example, from "To My Soul (2)": "And what we had / gave way like coffee grains / brushed across paper"—Valentine constructs a barely shimmering world, not really luminous at all, but rather occupying that space of the half-lit interior of the mosque. where one does not really have to strain to see, but merely wait until one's eyes adjust to the darkness and open space.[10] Sound and sense do push against each other, but meet here in the halfway place:

> But to you now I offer—forgive me, River—
> What I could never then, give over.[11]

NOTES

1. Jean Valentine, *Door in the Mountain: New and Collected Poems* (Middletown, CT: Wesleyan University Press, 2004), 13.

2. Ibid., 20.

3. Ibid., 56.

4. Ibid., 247.

5. Ibid., 261.

6. Ibid., 257.

7. Ibid., 137.

8. Ibid., 217.

9. Ibid., 29.

10. Jean Valentine, *Little Boat* (Middletown, CT: Wesleyan University Press, 2007), 64.

11. Ibid., 42.

Poetry and Community

It is hard to be brave or working all the time for social justice: I did it myself for four years after graduating from college, working on numerous issues, ranging from winning greater state and national support for public higher education systems to pressuring Congress to stop supporting the U.S.-backed Taliban government in Afghanistan.

But there is something personal, secretive, something inside that yearns for expression. I was getting up and speaking in front of crowds of hundreds, sometimes thousands, but found myself unable to say the most basic human things to the people around me, to the people I loved. It cost me, I can't even say out loud how much.

It's for this reason I have always been attracted to a very particular type of poem within June Jordan's body of work. A brave woman herself, working tirelessly, traveling to Central America during the brutal 1980s, teaching generations of students first at SUNY Stony Brook and then at UC Berkeley, and finally developing a pedagogy of liberation through her "Poetry for the People" project, Jordan is widely known and acclaimed as a political writer and political poet.

It's her lyrical writing I love, sometimes separate small love poems and fragments, but sometimes in moments within longer performative pieces, Jordan gives voice to the secret inside, the self that doesn't proclaim or declaim itself but still lives, tenderly, inside interior spaces.

"Of Faith: Confessional" begins, "silence polishing the streets to rain / who walk the waters / side by side."[1] Immediately we are atmospheric, the absolutely abstract "silence" acting upon the physical to yield phenomena. Later in the poem the same motion happens again: "tomorrow drums the body into birth." These results are seen "rioting" in the poet's awareness but are preferred to a more primitive understanding that "made dog eat dog / that made man smash man." The ruin of meaning leads, though, to a possible starting point. Jordan's line breaks and assonance bring much pleasure:

> catastrophe
>
> far better
> better bones
>
> establishing
>
> a second starting
> history
>
> a happiness

When one is constantly speaking for others or to others, it is sometimes hard to return to the lyrical and individual voice. After all, wouldn't the move toward political or public language necessarily overwhelm the individual lyric voice? Jordan herself, in a poem aptly titled "Poem to the Mass Communications Media," writes, "I will to be // I have begun // I am speaking // for my self."[2] I appreciate the double-spaced lines as a mode of bringing dramatic pause and silence into the poem as much as I appreciate the more conceptual gesture of separating the words "my self."

The engine for an individual's actions in the world can come from ego, the desire to remake situations to one's own desire, or it can come from empathy, a recognition of the connection between all sentient beings and a genuine selfless desire to improve conditions for others. Oftentimes, though she is most well-known for her political and declamatory poems, Jordan turns her attention inward.

Her heartbreaking poem "One Minus One Minus One" carries a short statement as an epigraph before the text of the poem: "This is a first map of territory / I will have to explore as poems, / again and again."[3] This idea that one will not be able

to finish the poem informs its own unfolding, to its moment of
lack of closure at its close:

> My mother murdering me
> to have a life of her own
>
> What would I say
> (if I could speak about it?)
>
> My father raising me
> to be a life that he
> owns
>
> What can I say
> (in this loneliness)

The poem shocks in its opening four words, and Jordan lets us
know in the first parenthetical that the speech act is purely condition, that she will not be able to actually do it. The father's
verb "raising" seems at first friendlier, until the dramatic repetition of the word "own" in a new context, a new grammatical
form (a verb now instead of a possessive) and with a new line
break that heightens its stark effect.

The final couplet is one of despair: the ability to speak is now
assumed (from "would" she says "can"), but even though she
now is able to speak, there is nothing she actually can speak of
in the loneliness brought about by her treatment. The poem
ends in a parenthetical, the possibility to speak compromised,
and the reader left to try to solve the sad arithmetic of the title.

Sometimes Jordan uses the compressed epigrammatic style
in service of a more subtle political commentary. Here is her
poem "Calling All Silent Minorities":

> HEY
> C'MON
> COME OUT
> WHEREVER YOU ARE
> WE NEED TO HAVE THIS MEETING
> AT THIS TREE
> AIN' EVEN BEEN
> PLANTED
> YET[4]

Her commitment is always toward building a community, but also simultaneously about how the individual finds herself in a community and about the ways necessary to sustain and build that community. June Jordan teaches us here, as Barack Obama famously quoted, "We are the ones we have been waiting for."[5]

Anne Waldman has dedicated much of her energy over her career to building links between various poetic communities, and also founding and helping to build strong, lasting institutions, among them the Poetry Project in New York City, and Naropa University in Colorado. Additionally, she has become an important part of the international poetry community. Her political work really privileges the importance of art as an instrument of social action and change, but also a deep commitment to spirituality and spiritual awakening.

As a poet and a performer, her sense of voice, body, and rhythm is sublime. Here's the very end of her long poem "Notes on Sitting Beside a Noble Corpse," an elegy for Allen Ginsberg:

> Allen Ginsberg will never embarrass China,
> Russia, the White House, dead corrupt
> presidents, Cuba, the C.I.A. Universe again
>
> But Allen Ginsberg will never ease the pain
> of living with human song & story again
> that's borne on wings of perpetual prophecy—
> life & death's a spiral!
> He's mounting the stairs now with Vajra Yogini[6]

The incantatory opening includes sharp humor with its "dead corrupt presidents," but also complete tenderness—"Allen Ginsberg will never ease the pain / of living with human song & story again." The rhythm of this stanza is also interrupted by the observation that "life and death's a spiral." The music that is made by the performance of the piece aloud allows us to participate in the mourning process like a ritual or a service. Waldman continues:

> Full Century's brilliant Allen's gone,
> in other myriad forms live on
> See through this palpable skull's tender eye,
> kind mind kind mind don't die!

This is language that actually *becomes* music, beginning with the staccato tempo of the first line transitioning to the smoothness of the second line, the third line with its alternating hard and soft consonants and the final line of punctuationless panic.

While Jordan oscillates dizzyingly and beautifully between a purely public address and the secret private moments of the interior heart, Waldman's poetry itself becomes a locus of connection between the individual and the world at large. But how does one continue the work of community building when one is removed completely from society as a whole? Marilyn Buck, a poet and translator who has spent more than twenty years in the federal prison system, writes of her experience, "Some prisoners resign themselves and stow their imagination in boxes labeled 'Open on release date' and bury themselves in the oblivion of prison culture, despair, religion or television."[7]

Some prisoners, Buck goes on to say, while inside the prison system, attempt to maintain their sense of individuality within a social structure at large, and not solely the prison itself as society. Prisoners like these, Buck says, "encounter possibility, imagination, desire—the substance of living" and "stockpile independence and nurture their uniqueness."

In the harrowing weeks following the September 11, 2001, terrorist attacks, Buck was removed from the prison population at large and placed in solitary confinement, ostensibly for her own protection. Buck, staunchly opposed to American imperialism at home and abroad, had been jailed for involvement with the Black Liberation Army. Though she has written various essays and political pieces about prison issues, it's her text "Incommunicado: Dispatches from a Political Prisoner" that tells the human story of her life in prison, while necessarily touching on the immediate political situation that led to her separation from the community at large.

While the other inmates watch the footage of the Trade Center buildings' collapse on television, Buck is in her cell, thinking, "I know / soon others will die / dark smoke spreads / cinders of wrath rise."[8] One of the other prisoners runs into her room and asks if they will shoot the political prisoners. Though Buck reassures her friend, she thinks, "(question marks / the corners of my mouth: / what do I know / about the fine-print)."

Ultimately, for the moment, there is no answer: "I turn to sweep the floor / find rhythms of the ordinary."

Several hours later that day, Buck is taken into solitary confinement, told it is for her own safety though she denies this is the case. "You're intelligent / you know why," she is told. "I keep outrage / wrapped within my fists," she writes. "I swallow anger / metal clangs swallow sound / the concrete cocoon swallows me." Six days later she receives two lifelines—a radio to listen to and communication from the women outside her solitary confinement cell; they begin yelling out to her and tapping on the wall so Buck knows they are there. "I swing hope on a thread," Buck writes. "I drop / frozen chrysalis / cold into a coffin box."

The "lifeline" of the radio is a double-edged sword; through it Buck hears of "Sikhs dead, detainees disappeared / political prisoners buried deeper / incommunicado." It's ironic that she herself is one of the last group, hanging from "a winding string / winding in this cocoon." Like the cocoon in nature, Buck, separated from her community twice now, must reach into her own self for resources: "I must seek cycles / inside / without clocks or mirrors / without all but I." By choosing the nominative "I" as her object rather than the grammatically correct "me," she asserts her essential selfhood, which is not, can never be, diminished by imprisonment or isolation.

She carries this lesson with her when on September 24 she is finally released, "a four o'clock unfolding, fuchsia in the shading light / back into the routine prisoner's plight."

Perhaps it is simply the *presence* of an individual asserting her selfhood in relationship to the polity at large that is the beginning of political action. Something like that happened, I think, in New York City after the events of September 11, 2001. Immediately afterward, while support for the war grew strong across the country, people in New York City itself began holding candlelight peace vigils in Union Square.

There also came a collective accumulation, a group sculpture—candles, letters, flowers, toys, prayers to the lost, notes written on posters, pictures of missing or lost people . . . A poster of a young Indian software designer taped to the streetlamp had an inscription written on it in magic marker: "We miss you, where are you?" Pat Brown, the firefighter who would shortly be featured in an issue of *Yoga Journal,* gazed serenely from a poster tacked up to the impromptu bulletin boards at Grand Central. After the issue hit the newsstands, someone wrote on the poster in red pen, "*Namaste,* Pat."

Our grief came in a wellspring of collective expression, at Union Square, at the arch in Washington Square, and at the boards in Grand Central. But it was at Union Square that the nightly peace vigils continued to take place and opposition to the war, promised at that time to be brief, continued to grow.

One day, as a friend was passing by, police officers arrived at Union Square to begin collecting all the memorial material, all the letters and notices, the candles and flowers. "Where are you taking this?" several passersby asked and were told, "It's all being archived." But it was taken away in clear trash bags without any care.

Soon after this Union Square was cordoned off, closed for renovations.

But peace as an expression is truly the natural state of humans. There can be no endless war. Art and poetry can both speak against death and speak of a commitment to life and to human understanding.

Layla Al-Attar, the Iraqi painter, was like this. Her beautiful paintings, stark and luminous at once, show reverence for the human form and the natural world. One painting shows a woman, nude, in the forest, in the moonlight, dissolving into the trees themselves, dissolving into the yellow-white light of the full moon.

Al-Attar too was politically engaged, speaking out actively against the still ongoing U.S. bombardment campaign of Iraq. Though the first Gulf War had ended a few years earlier, the U.S. was still targeting military installations in Iraq. Frequently these missiles were hitting civilian targets, and Al-Attar was active in the campaign to call attention to these deaths. She was quite a public figure as an artist also, representing Iraq at the Venice Biennale, receiving medals and citations for her work from the governments of Poland and Kuwait and serving as director of the national gallery in Baghdad.

I would give anything for you to not know already how the story ends.

The individual body does die. Death takes brilliance with it. Art and poetry fold quickly under fire from the sky, under power exercised. The paintings that were and which could have been mix together as cinders and drift away in the wind.

How does one continue to work through the state of despair? After a time, it ceases to be despair, and becomes only work—a commitment to peace and to peaceful methods of achieving it. Rachel Tzvia Back, a poet living in Western Galilee and involved in various Israeli peace movements, writes about it in her poem "Notes: from the Wait":

> You are right to stay away
> Those prayers on the doorpost
> will protect no one
>
> As to why we remain:
> we're busy now
> waiting
>
> behind bolted doors
> for the season that will not pass
> to pass[9]

NOTES

1. June Jordan, *Directed by Desire* (Port Townsend, WA: Copper Canyon Press, 2005), 70.

2. Ibid., 71.

3. Ibid., 202.

4. Ibid., 149.

5. Ibid., 279.

6. Anne Waldman, "Notes on Sitting Beside a Noble Corpse," Jehat .com, http://www.jehat.com/Jehaat/en/Poets/Anne.htm (accessed August 15, 2009).

7. Marilyn Buck, introduction to *State of Exile*, by Cristina Peri Rossi (San Francisco: City Lights Books, 2008), xi.

8. Marilyn Buck, "Incommunicado: Dispatches from a Political Prisoner," Prisonactivist.org, http://www.prisonactivist.org/archive/pps+ pows/marilynbuck/Incommunicado.html (accessed August 6, 2009).

9. Rachel Tzvia Back, *Azimuth,* Sheep Meadow Press.

Poetry Is Dangerous

On April 19, 2007, after a day of teaching classes at Shippensburg University, I went out to my car and grabbed a box of old poetry manuscripts from the front seat of my little white beetle and carried it across the street and put it next to the trash can outside Wright Hall. The poems were from poetry contests I had been judging, and the box was heavy. I had previously left my recycling boxes there, and they were always picked up and taken away by the trash department.

A young man from ROTC was watching me as I got into my car and drove away. I thought he was looking at my car, which has black flower decals along its sides and sometimes inspires strange looks. I later discovered that I, in my dark skin, am sometimes not even a person to the people who look at me. Instead, in spite of my peacefulness, my committed opposition to all aggression and war, I am a threat by my very existence, a threat just living in the world as a Muslim body.

Upon my departure, he alerted the police. He told them a man of Middle Eastern descent driving a heavily decaled white beetle with out-of-state plates and no campus parking sticker had just placed a box next to the trash can. My car has NY plates, but he got the rest of it wrong. I have two stickers on my car. One is my highly visible faculty parking sticker, and the other, which I just don't have the heart to take off these days, says "Kerry/Edwards: For a Stronger America."

Because of my recycling the bomb squad came, the state police came. Because of my recycling buildings were evacuated, classes were canceled, campus was closed. No. Not because of my recycling. Because of my dark body. No. Not because of my dark body. Because of his fear. Because of the way he saw me. Because of the culture of fear, mistrust, hatred and suspicion that is carefully cultivated in the media, by the government, by people who claim to want to keep us "safe."

These are the days of orange alert, school lockdowns and endless war. We are preparing for it, training for it, looking for it, and so of course, in the most innocuous of places—a professor wanting to hurry home, hefting his box of discarded poetry—we find it.

That man in the parking lot didn't even see me. He saw my darkness. He saw my Middle Eastern descent. Ironic because though my ancestry is indeed Middle Eastern, I am Indian and look it; I've never been mistaken for a Middle Eastern man by anyone who'd ever met one.

One of my colleagues was in the gathering crowd, trying to figure out what had happened. She heard my description—a Middle Eastern man driving a white beetle with out-of-state plates—and knew immediately they were talking about me and realized that the box must have been manuscripts I was discarding. She approached them and told them I was a professor on the faculty there. Immediately the campus police officer said, "What country is he from?"

"What country is he from?!" she yelled, indignant.

"Ma'am, you are associated with the suspect. You need to step away and lower your voice," he told her.

At some length several of my faculty colleagues were able to get through to the police and get me on a cell phone. I explained to the university president, who was on the scene, and then to the state police that the box contained old poetry manuscripts that needed to be recycled. The police officer told me that in the current climate I needed to be more careful about how I behaved. "When I recycle?" I asked.

The university president appreciated my distress about the situation but denied that the call had anything to do with my race or ethnic background. The spokesperson for the university called it an "honest mistake," referring not to the young man from ROTC giving in to his worst instincts and calling the police but to me, who made the mistake of being dark skinned and putting my recycling next to the trash can.

The university's bizarrely minimal statement lets everyone know that the "suspicious package" beside the trash can ended up being, indeed, trash. It goes on to say, "We appreciate your co-operation during the incident and remind everyone that safety is a joint effort by all members of the campus community."

What does that community mean to me, a person who has to walk by the ROTC offices every day on my way to my own office just down the hall—who was watched, noted and reported, all in a day's work? Today we gave in willingly and wholeheartedly to a culture of fear and blaming and profiling. It is deemed perfectly appropriate behavior to spy on one another and police one another and report on one another. Such behaviors exist most strongly in closed and undemocratic and fascist societies.

The university report does not mention the root cause of the alarm. That package became "suspicious" because of who was holding it, who put it down, who drove away. Me.

It was poetry, I kept insisting to the state policeman who was questioning me on the phone. It was poetry I was putting out to be recycled.

My body exists politically in a way I cannot prevent. For a moment today, without even knowing it, driving away from campus in my little beetle, exhausted after a day of teaching, listening to Justin Timberlake on the radio, I ceased to be a person when a man I had never met looked straight through me and saw the violence in his own heart.

The Architecture of Loneliness

One wishes to say that the construction of an entire cathedral inside the Great Mosque of Córdoba during the reign of King Charles I of Spain was one of the greatest cultural crimes of history, on par with the destruction of the Great Library of Alexandria or the Temple of Solomon, but it's not really true, since of the first nothing at all remains and of the second the last remaining vestige—the Wailing Wall—has somehow metonymically *become* the temple itself, reservoir for the prayers—intangible words but also physically realized in bits of paper thrust into the cracks in the physical structure itself—for countless generations. The mosque, or the Cathedral of Córdoba as it is now known, still exists, but in its defaced form, endless acres of empty galleries and pillars, and right when you think you've achieved a nirvana of space: a cathedral—yes, right there, a sixteenth-century cathedral with all the trappings—*inside* the unspeakably gigantic mosque.

Space is all I had, haunting the coast road between Toulouse and Granada like a ghost across three suppressed kingdoms, whose languages, cities, populations diminished over the centuries and finally dispersed into smoke. At one end of the line, Carcassonne, once a stronghold of the disappeared Cathar religion, stands as a carnival-city, nearly perfectly preserved in its eleventh-century form because its inhabitants were flushed out and exterminated. The city itself lay vacant and covered with the debris of nearly a millennium before being excavated and restored to "authenticity."

At the other end, the cities of the old Western caliphate and Muslim kingdoms, abandoned by their ghosts, seek now actively to attract them back to the old haunts. The feeling of loss and longing for an absent homeland in the literature of the expelled Jews and Muslims of Spain finds gruesome counterpart in the commercialization and fetishizing of that exile for the tourist industry in Andalucía. Thousands of tourists a day pay and pay to tramp through the Alhambra in Granada, the Alcazaba of Málaga, the Alcázar of Sevilla—though this last was built in the Muslim style by a Christian king utilizing many of the same Muslim craftsmen who designed and built the more famous Alhambra.

A whole tourist industry sustains the economy of Andalucía, once called Al-Andalus, despite nearly three hundred years of religious, social and architectural efforts to completely eradicate any trace of the non-Christian from Spain. Disconcertingly but gloriously, many of Spain's North African and Middle Eastern immigrants are moving back into the old Muslim quarters. After nearly 520 years, Granada's Albaycin neighborhood once again echoes with the call to prayer broadcast from the newly constructed mosque.

But is what we've left behind as real as we think? Generations of Sephardim, traumatized by yet another exile, passed down through the years keys to their old houses in Toledo. As poignant a metaphor as the Wailing Wall, the keys themselves *became* exile physically personified—keys to buildings that perhaps or perhaps not have themselves ceased to exist, keys that might or might not open anything anymore. Home is perhaps *impossible*, or more to the point, the key itself, the houseless key, became the state of exile.

"Enter them so we may exit completely," wrote Mahmoud Darwish about the abandoned homes of Andalucía in his poem sequence "Eleven Stars over Andalusia," sensitively translated by Agha Shahid Ali. That replacement is almost required to make the exile total; if a place is made into metaphor, the wanderer has a shot of keeping his home alive and in his pocket. As Darwish goes on to say, "Soon we will search in the margins of your history / for what was once *our* history . . . Was Andalusia here or there? On the land . . . or in the poems?"[1]

It's a heartbreaking question—how long do you keep alive the dream of returning home? Cristina Peri Rossi, a Uruguayan poet who in 1972 fled the military junta to Barcelona, writes in her book *The State of Exile*, "If exile were not a terrible human experience, it would be a literary genre." And quickly adds, "Or both things at the same time."[2]

What one has left behind stops being the actual point. The condition of loss and loneliness becomes more real than what was left behind, not important for its own self, but only for the fact that it has been left, is no longer, can no longer be, home. Peri Rossi wonders, "Did there exist once a city called Montevideo?"[3]

Neither the temple in Jerusalem nor the Mosque of Córdoba can ever really be restored, not the way anyone thinks. Not the least reason is that they both already currently exist in states altered by war and history. Peri Rossi says, "Partir / es siempre partirse en dos"—"To depart / is always to split oneself in two."[4]

This is the first urge for the exile, toward language of course—whether it is the Chinese poetry scratched into the wood at the Angel Island immigration center in San Francisco, poetry the Guantánamo inmates wrote into foam cups or the poetry immortalized by Dan Pagis in his poem "line written in pencil in the sealed railway car." His brief, immortal poem runs in its entirety, *"here in this carload / I am eve / with abel my son / if you see my other son / cain son of man / tell him that i"*[5]

It's that final "i," both lowercase and without verb or final punctuation, that breaks the heart. It speaks to the interruption at the conclusion of the poem, the interruption of the speaker's ability to write, the implied interruption of her life, but also actually empowers that final "i" to become both noun and verb, to become the final actor on the stage of the poem, to assert itself, no matter how desperately, to exist, to be human and real. "How I love you, you who have broken me, string by string, on the road to her heated night," insists Darwish. "Sing how, after you, the smell of coffee has no morning."[6]

These moments—the simple ones, the quotidian ones—are the ones carried into exile. The landscape of the new country becomes a metaphor for loss of the old. When Picasso left Andalusia, for example, first for Barcelona and then Paris, it was always an Andalusian landscape that haunted the canvas.

Of course in Barcelona, famously of the blue skies and cool nights, birthplace of Modernisme, one would expect to see the organic forms of the wind and water—in Miró, in Dalí, in Tapiés, and Picasso—mirrored in the concrete forms, not just in the cathedral and buildings of Gaudí, but in the natural world also, in the slopes of Montserrat and gardens of Montjuic. When is a balcony not a balcony? When it's a pelvic bone.

My favorite part of the Sagrada Familia cathedral is the wall from which birds ripple up and break free. Well, maybe that's a close second to the statue of Jesus being kissed by Judas near the main doors. Really it's the look on Jesus's face—heartbroken, knowing he's being betrayed but committed to living out his fate to be a sacrifice, full of pity for Judas and for what comes after. Oh, but what I'm really in love with is those impossible doors, littered, inscribed to the point of ridiculous graffiti with language, scripture, mathematical symbols, equations, geometric patterns—the purest minimalist gone crazy over excess. That's Gaudí to me, an orgasm of form, all riveted together by the most solemn things—that look on Jesus's face, the little sudoku anagram embedded in the door—no matter which way you add the numbers, they come up to thirty-three.

Always in the experience of exile, secrets that are kept, an individual in a foreign land, trying to remember how to pronounce the syllables of her language, trying to remember how to say her own name. Peri Rossi writes in her foreword to *State of Exile:* "Only when the exile is collective—from the very remote, such as that of the Jewish Diaspora, to the exile of Spaniards faithful to the Republic—is part of the identity preserved in spite of the change in place. Then its symbols become charged with significance—from the flags to the hymns, from the cuisine to the style of dress, the mating rituals to the dance steps. They are no longer commonplace, they become roots, anchors, emblems."[7]

And when things become haunted with their old significance, the exiled one becomes trapped in a semiotics of stagnation. "Dusk still falls rose-drenched / there are young girls who would like to be doves / but they must go to school," she writes.[8] The nostalgia itself paralyzes one in time, utterly removed from the experience of place, "as if everything in the world / had happened to us already, forever."[9]

She doesn't want to leave us at that moment though, fractured, exiled, depressed. She reaches for her new life in Barcelona, saying, "I think in loving you / I shall learn a new tongue."[10] In fact, her exile has brought her homeland into even sharper relief. She says, "To remember / I had to leave."[11] She later concludes, when the military junta collapses and Uruguay is democratic again and she decides she will not return, "Ithaca exists / as long as you never go back."[12]

The last time I went to Barcelona, I went below the streets of the city into the ancient, newly excavated Roman portions. Imagine being human under the ground, in ancient spaces, and not culturally grand spaces but ordinary places—a laundry, a *garum* factory, a dyeing facility. On my road to and then through Andalucía, I tried to go underground into the ancient ruins as often as I could. I wanted to understand that cities are what's under the surface, that the visible buildings are only consonants of a city's language. As with language, one has to learn the vowels to be able to speak—the vowels meaning the empty spaces of silence in the words and in the human body that makes them, the streets and buildings underneath the streets and buildings that you see.

In Valencia I saw it. The buildings themselves were magnificent non sequiturs—a Modernist building next to something from the nineteenth century, the bullring up against a modern bank building. The city gates still stand, though the walls are demolished. The gates themselves, marked by Napoleon's cannonballs, lead you down a crooked road to a little plaza—a plaza that has always been there, served the same purpose, even in Roman times. There, beneath the glass-floored fountain, are the ruins of the old Roman baths. If you go down the stairs, the ruins stretch for acres in every direction and from every era, the first city, the second city, Roman, Arab. Cities lie on top of cities, sometimes replacing them but more often occupying exactly the same space as them, cathedrals on top of mosques on top of churches on top of temples.

When space is so crushed in such a situation, something happens to one's sense of time as well. Isn't, even after five hundred and some years, Granada still fundamentally the Muslim city it has always been? How is it everything happens so quickly?

Yannis Ritsos wrote the short book *The Negatives of Silence* over the course of one month in the summer of 1987. He'd taken notes and written toward the poems over the course of the preceding year, and after the month of intense writing set about another month of revising and completing the book. Far from suffering from the intense pace of the creation, the poems seem *forged* in it. This rush of composition seems shared by the intense poetry of exile. The poems themselves speak of loneliness, but a loneliness borne of exclusion from the larger whole: "You sense you are not invited / to these public festivities. So you sit / alone, waiting for night, hoping the stars / will resume, by means of secret signals, / your private sacraments, light years away."[13]

The poet is not quite lonely due to the fact of exclusion but because he cannot yet send the "private sacraments."

Ritsos's loneliness, like Peri Rossi's, seems not tied to exile itself, but rather an intrinsic condition of the heart. Ritsos's response is an exquisitely rendered attempt at descriptions: little scenes, domestic, tender, that nonetheless fall apart in face of the terrifying void. When, in "Eleven Planets," Darwish seems most in crisis, it's not the symbols, hymns and flags he remembers, but rather the smallest and most domestic things: "In the exodus I love you more, / I empty my soul of words. . . . In exodus / we remember the lost buttons of our shirts, we forget / the crown of our days, we remember the apricot's sweat, we forget / the dance of horses on festival nights."[14]

In "Minimal Harvest," Ritsos tries to render a similarly domestic scene, but in his penultimate line, "A young girl comes up the hill carrying a basket of mulberries," comes to a point of failure—how to make something of experience? He cannot and continues, "Leave it at that: the hill, the young girl, a basket of mulberries."[15] One feels the exhaustion of his spiritual resources. Throughout the poems, the poet is too tired to notice, is unable to see or speak to people. One thinks of the keys of Toledo—one is too tired to do anything other than carry the keys—the keys which may open nothing after all, but are all one has left of the homeland.

In a poem titled "Useless Keys," Ritsos writes of a pile of keys found on the table. One of the keys is "this little silver one . . . it's to that jewelry box . . . that fell down the well years ago. / They drained the well, searched. They found / nothing, only rocks."[16] Despite the fact that nothing was found of the treasure in the well, the key remains, remains with all the others.

The poems too are full of absent places, empty suitcases, postmen that don't call, doors that slam shut, all images of loneliness and separation. Ritsos is always sitting still—it's everyone around him that is always leaving. In this state of loneliness, he becomes aware that his world is losing significance, looking at "a plume of smoke, held still, trying to bestow / some nonexistent meaning on us and on the world. / Ah—to think that silent beauty no longer takes us in."[17]

Ultimately, perhaps we are more attached to the key itself rather than to what it might open. In fact, a key to nowhere is even better. In the empty spaces, in the "silent beauty," we might even have a shot at finding ourselves.

For this reason, in Málaga I could only stand and gape at the cathedral. Like a lot of cathedrals in that part of Spain, it was built on top of what used to be a mosque. It was awful in its Baroque magnificence, and it was perfect for one reason only: the south tower was never built. It climbs a little way up and then just stops at empty sky. It's that second tower, the one that was never built, that's the reason this place is a way to god, I suddenly thought.

Not like the tower which collapsed, the punishment for the building of which was the splintering of our original language into tongues.

That's really the Muslim in me—entranced by the empty space of the sky or the wide interior of the mosque of Córdoba. I'd almost always rather have empty space and silence than an icon or bell, almost always rather have language in my mouth than transubstantiated body or blood.

The architectural violence done in Córdoba—the demolishing of the center of the interior of the mosque to construct the cathedral—is mirrored in the curatorial violence of the visitors' guide entitled "The Cathedral of Córdoba," rendering any history of the building as a Muslim site of worship in the solid past tense, framing its existence as a mosque—for nearly three hundred years—as an "interruption" of the site's history as a Christian place of worship, neglecting to mention that the church previously on the site willingly shared its space with Córdoba's growing Muslim community and then later sold its building to the Muslims when it became clear they needed a larger space, neglecting also to mention that many churches were themselves built on top of pagan temples. As if to emphasize the current re-framing of the mosque as an interruption in the intrinsic Christian nature of the site, part of the floor has been permanently exposed, a large window revealing the excavated floor of the old Visigothic church below.

Then again, people still largely believe some of history's more fabulous lies: that a Muslim army destroyed the Great Library of Alexandria (false), that Harry S. Truman believed that the deployment of atomic weapons against Hiroshima and Nagasaki would save the lives of American combat troops (the truth is much more complicated and admitted to be so by Truman himself in his autobiography) and that the intent of the 2004 invasion of Iraq was to root out the hidden weapons of mass destruction (no comment). There is, of course, no final exam in History.

At any rate, the Mezquita, or "mosque," as it is colloquially known by Córdobans—a friend said in casual conversation, "My grandfather used to go to mass at the mosque"—has been consecrated as a church for as much time or more than it had been a mosque before, so how can one complain about it? One might complain, however, that unlike in its previous incarnation as a Visigothic church, these days it is literally forbidden for Muslims to pray there. Which didn't stop me.

Who am I to pray, at odds with orthodoxy? Perennially confused, I haven't uttered prayers in years, but neither have I ever decided I wasn't Muslim. There in that space, where prayer is expressly forbidden, I—who am also, in a certain fashion, forbidden—found myself in a most curious position: it wasn't that I *should* pray, obligated by my faith, but that this place, vexed and altered, was perhaps the only place I *could*—and more than that, much more—it was only *me*, of the dozens of Muslims who were in the building at the time, who could.

That vexed place, the once-mosque now very stridently not-a-mosque, for me became the only possible mosque, an exile in a structure of loss and loneliness, a Jew at the remaining wall, the site of my very faith an interrupted, displaced, transposed place, I its only possible believer.

Of course it was a secret prayer—uttered under my breath

and without the ritual bows and prostrations normally required. Such adaptations to circumstance, like nominal conversions and even denials of faith, are perfectly permissible according to circumstance in Islamic tradition.

But it feels a little bit of a tragedy, to assert oneself only in secret. How many languages were forgotten, how many names were changed?

It's much more complicated when one brings one's state of exile to a space of cultural blankness, where one is always expected to either generate one's own resources of culture, or adapt to a prefab reality that exists in a cultureless vacuum of strip malls, suburbs and flat-screen televisions. Nowhere was this more apparent than in the days just after September 11, 2001. As Slavoj Žižek discusses extensively in his book *Welcome to the Desert of the Real,* we had a moment of experiencing a "real" event, but rather than actually engage it, actually experience it, we downloaded our reality onto remote targets once again, in this case Iraq and Afghanistan, and once more—nearly pathologically—got on with business as usual.

On September 19, 2001, Semezdin Mehmedinovic, a Bosnian poet who came the U.S. as a political refugee in 1996, took a train trip across the country from Virginia to California and back. As he went from city to city—an exile of war now witnessing the opening of another one—he explored ideas of rootlessness in one sequence, ideas of home in a second, both written in short periods like Ritsos's work, written in moments of isolation itself.

Like Peri Rossi, Mehmedinovic *wants* to find a new home and an end to actual, if not metaphorical, exile in the new nation. Leaving his new hometown of Alexandria, Virginia, he writes, "There are at least nine cities in America called Alexandria. / Cartography of the new had to be based on the / Principle of tracing the old world / Through an ocean of indigo . . ."[18] He realizes, it seems, that *no* city is "real"; each is only a collection of expectations generated by the people who come to it. "The only thing that makes / My trip across country imaginable is this," he goes on to say. "Going from one Alexandria to another / I can't help but get to the same city."

Is it this knowledge then, that "the world is still in one piece," that gives him an anchor to hold on to through the journey and the disorienting weeks that followed?

They were surreal weeks indeed—news polls were reporting that 90 percent of Americans supported military action against Afghanistan and over 50 percent supported forced internment of recent Arab American immigrants. And, most bizarrely, in addition to voting 534-1 in favor of granting the president full power to carry out his attack on Afghanistan, the U.S. Congress appeared on national television to sing "God Bless America." I do not know if Barbara Lee, the sole vote against military action, also joined in the singing. On October 14, seven days into the military action, the Taliban government offered to surrender Bin Laden for trial. The offer was refused by President Bush, who denied there was a need for trial.[19]

The flag, for any community, becomes a symbol for lost values. They are necessarily "lost" because if they were actually culturally present there would be no need for the metaphorical reminder. It's a thought along the lines of classical Islamic prohibitions against depicting the face of God or of prophets: that an image degrades or diminishes the original. Furthermore, one mistrusts a symbol without clearly articulated represented values: "Truth, justice and the American way" doesn't quite explain enough. The first two qualities are claimed by most nations that have taken such a designation for themselves, and the third only names a quality by way of adjective; it doesn't explain.

But, as Etel Adnan writes, "Contrary to what is usually believed, it is not general ideas and a grandiose unfolding of great events that most impress the mind in times of heightened historic upheavals but, rather, it is the uninterrupted flow of little experiences, observations, disturbances, small ecstasies, or barely perceptible discouragements that up the trivialized day-to-day living."[20] Darwish knows the lesson: "One day I'll pass [Granada's] moons / and brush my desire against a lemon tree . . . Embrace me and let me be reborn."[21]

To Mehmedinovic, exiled from his own country even as it began seceding into its constituent parts, traveling across the vastness of another country, built out of similarly disparate pieces, flags make no actual sense. To him, "a flag exists only / As the wind's unadulterated intention."[22] To unify the ideals of a nation into one symbol is not only impossible, but dangerous. I saw it in Spain: the national project of the Catholic monarchs of 1492 was to literally *create* a Spanish national identity out of all the disparate kingdoms on the peninsula. To this day, even after Franco's forty-year effort last century, it hasn't worked—Spain has four national languages; two entire regions that have active separatist movements; and several regions, including Catalunya, that have unique autonomous status with their own governing parliaments. Andalucía, far from being cleansed of its Arab influences after three hundred years of concerted, state-sponsored effort, seems positively and inescapably haunted by it, culturally, architecturally, socially.

The idea of fixing history, especially one's own history, is a fraught enterprise. On the train, Mehmedinovic spies a fellow passenger's Quran and muses, "Readers search for a 'critical edition' / That will resolve all the / Difficulties of ambiguous lines."[23] It's impossible, he knows. The thorny images, wild non sequiturs, repetitions, re-telling of stories with both cosmetic and substantive differences—they're hallmarks of the Quran, not difficulties in understanding it, but actually *modes* to entering the text at all. "Clouds retreat before such queries," writes Mehmedinovic. "Stars illuminate new worlds."

Mehmedinovic's sense of strangeness in the new land is total, but equals at least his experience of strangeness in the old one—he claims, "I plainly lack the gift of / dividing memories of home from the house itself."[24] This is Peri Rossi's gift, Darwish's gift, when he says, "Palestine is not only Palestine but exists in an aesthetic realm much vaster," which is to say it is a type and site of human loneliness.

Isn't Palestine now like the Mezquita in Córdoba? A place with another place inside, not possible to exist except in the tense of memory? One might suggest that Israel itself was able to transcend its existence as memory and metaphor and actualize itself, but its existence has gone hand in hand, since the beginning, with the vexed relationship with Palestine. And Darwish longs for more than mere metaphor of place when he writes, "I do not want a place to be buried in / I want a place to live in and to curse if I want."[25] As it is now physically impossible to have a Mezquita without the cathedral in its center, impossible to have the cathedral without the surrounding Mezquita, it might too be impossible spiritually or metaphysically to have one nation without the other. They depend on one another for actual existence.

And honestly—though perhaps I am being naïve—why couldn't the Catholic Church open the nineteen sealed doors of the Mezquita, abolish the eight-euro entrance fee and once again permit Muslim worship inside? The struggle for sovereignty over the space could be surrendered to history, the building itself surrendered as a "monument," and be once more a part of living, actual life—tombstone no more but actual building. My friend asked every security guard he could find about the notion; they all seemed uniformly nonplussed.

Just five minutes walking from the Mezquita, tucked away in a tangle of crooked streets surging flush against the old city wall, you will find the old Jewish Quarter of Córdoba. So ordinary you would miss it, just past a little courtyard with a statue of Musa Ibn Mahmoun—you know him as Maimonides—you find an old thirteenth-century synagogue, the only remaining synagogue in all of Andalucía from the days of the Sefared. It is free to go inside and tiny—so small, startling to realize how small the congregation must have been, but then one remembers there were countless synagogues all across the quarter and the city. Startling also to see the classical Arabic architecture and geometric designs in the stonework, so like a mosque in every way, but with one striking and incredibly beautiful difference: the calligraphy inside is Hebrew.

The expulsion was momentous and shattered Spanish society as its highest levels, as an entire class of educated thinkers, scholars, teachers and writers were forced out of their professions and out of the country. Queen Isabel's chancellor, a Jew, was completely powerless to prevent the expulsion but managed a last metaphorical act, a poetic gesture most resonant: the day the act of expulsion went into effect was the same day on the Jewish calendar as the destruction of the Temple.[26]

And so hundreds of thousands of people left behind their homes and wealth—conveniently confiscated by the bankrupted throne—taking with them only what they could carry, and secreted away in their clothes and bags some of them took with them their keys to the sky.

In addition to the thirteenth-century synagogue in Córdoba, there are only two other synagogues in all of Spain (both in Toledo) left from the time of Sefared. One of them, the Sinagoga Transito, has been transformed into a museum of Jewish culture. It is somewhat surreal, looking at the dusty exhibits of shirts and spoons and old manuscript books behind glass. "It's like they are completely removed from history," my partner Marco said to me.

In the case of the Muslims who are not permitted to pray in the Mezquita, it seems almost the reverse. In Granada, the Alhambra is responsible for nearly all the tourism—countless restaurants, cafés, bars and even brands of alcohol take their names from the palace on the hill. My favorite poster was of a young mullah-type, turban and all, holding his beer. The caption in Spanish read something like, "I know it's against scripture, but what flavor!" The castle itself is a tomb—ornate, unspeakably beautiful and utterly empty. Crowds of tourists file through, touching the walls, the tile-work, the doors. It's been gorgeously restored. History of the expelled is fine so long as its tense is past-perfect.

There are two cruel gifts of the Cathedral of Córdoba; the first is of course that it exists at all. The great mosque of Sevilla has been completely destroyed. Only two small parts of it remain. The first is the minaret, though it has been capped by a sixteenth-century-style bell tower. The fusion of the Arab architecture with the Spanish cap is a strange though seemingly more harmonious reenactment of the fusion in the Mezquita. The second part of the mosque of Sevilla that was preserved is, beautifully, its courtyard. That only the empty space—though of critical importance; it was here that worshipers would engage in ritual ablutions—is preserved seems appropriate.

The second strange gift is that the "fusion" of the Mezquita may be a fact of life, but in the iconography of the building it's barely happened. In images, the addition/imposition of the cathedral is completely ignored. On the postcards, commemorative plaques and ceramic plates, only the empty aisles of the mosque, the ubiquitous red and white double arches, are depicted, nary a stitch or pillar of the cathedral or Christian images to be seen.

Of course, the imposition of one place onto another never goes down easy. No one knows this better than Mahmoud Darwish, whose birthplace and childhood home of Birweh doesn't exist anymore. Darwish's family returned to Israel after the war of 1948 to find the village was one of those that was completely demolished. As villages and towns in Israel/Palestine each have two names, one in Hebrew and one in Arabic, the two religions share countless symbols and traditions. My favorite is the silver amulet of a hand, which Jews call the "hand of Miriam" and which Shi'a take as a symbol for the Ahl-e-Bait, the family of the prophet.

That is the tragedy then—to be unable to agree on the meaning of a symbol. To be a person without a place, a believing mortal body in a world that passes. This land—Spain—with a history of nearly a thousand years, sought to eradicate all traces of itself and sent its citizens to be scattered, without papers in another landscape, rejected from the belief in Nation or God.

Who do you cling to then? No one knows a country like those exiled from it, and no one knows god like those expelled from paradise. Clutching keys to houses in Toledo for half a millennium, the primary condition of a person excluded from history or paradise is loneliness. It's not loneliness for the country or god left behind, because the very fact of exile has convinced you that it was never yours to begin with. Rather, one realizes a deeper loneliness, profound, that lives in the heart of the human and cannot be succored.

This duress, the spiritual strain, is responsible for the pace of writing—Ritsos's sequences written in a month, Mehmedinovic's written during the train trip, Peri Rossi's on the boat from Uruguay to Barcelona and in the months that followed. As Peri Rossi's translator, Marilyn Buck, notes, in the U.S. we are in a continuing condition of internal exile, certain populations excluded from the polity—Japanese Americans literally during the internment; Arab Americans in the days, months and years following 9/11; Native Americans in every way through American history. And of course, unlike in Spain where official documents and public signage frequently appear in multiple languages, monolingual Spanish speakers in the United States face exclusion and discrimination based solely on their language ability, cloaked in racist rhetoric of national origin and immigrant status. Illegal English-language and European immigrants are not similarly targeted.

It is almost laughable to think about our "pluralistic" nation's attitude toward language when I think back on the day I became hopelessly lost in Valencia because in my tour book the maps had all Spanish street names, when in the city the signs had all been switched to Valenciano, a dialect of Catalán.

And how do you go home, I've always wondered, when all the street signs have been changed? When the junta folded, Peri Rossi herself had to make the decision whether or not to return to her "Ithaca": "I did not want to repeat the experience of longing. I do not want to feel a different nostalgia. I prefer to hold on to the same one. I have lived with it, I do not want to live with others."[27] She remained in Barcelona, where she lives still. Though the poems from *State of Exile* were written quickly, she withheld them from publication for nearly thirty years. Perhaps they themselves were her key to the house in Toledo. She could not surrender them to the world without truly accepting that the exile was permanent, that return was impossible, that it could never be undone. In this way, publication is the final acceptance of that loneliness.

Of her decision to publish the poems, Peri Rossi wrote, "Thirty years are nothing, or they are an eternity. I'll bet on both." One finds oneself, always, like Ritsos, in writing. In fact, like a confused Muslim in the confounded Mezquita, it's in writing only that an exile is perhaps able to find himself.

While I was in Córdoba, remembering my prayers and trying to tell one brick apart from another, Mahmoud Darwish, the poet laureate of loneliness if there ever was one, passed away. Because he was so desperately in love with the world, its flowers, its burdens, its olive trees and its drunkenness, I could barely speak. With a numb mouth, I tried reciting his lines, ones I've carried in my own heart since reading them. In his book *Memory for Forgetfulness,* written in France after he fled the siege of Beirut in 1982, he mused on the most ordinary of things. While on his hands and knees crawling through the hallway of his apartment, listening to bombs destroying the floors above him, he yearns: "I want nothing more from the passing days than the aroma of coffee . . . so I can hold myself together, stand on my feet, and be transformed from something that crawls, into a human being . . . Coffee is the sister of time."[28] Is it possible to feel so lost that one doesn't exist anymore?

In Darwish's meditation on loneliness in place, "Not as a Foreign Tourist Does," the speaker, walking "on what remains of the heart," sees a girl in a field reading "what / looks like poetry."[29] He immediately feels that if he were either older ("the wolf would have surrendered to me") or younger ("I would have . . . taught her how to touch the rainbow"), he would be able to be present in the moment with her, but in his current condition he is unable to. Instead he walks, "as a foreign tourist does . . . / a camera with me, and my guide a little book / containing poems that describe this place / by a few foreign poets." For a moment one feels Darwish is criticizing the notion of experiencing the place not through the girl—the real existing place—but instead in the poems. However, he goes on to say, "I feel as if I were the speaker in them / and had it not been for the difference in rhyme / I would have said: / I am another." It's *real* for him then, the experience of the place through poetry—in the case of Palestine, perhaps more real than in the actuality itself. Al-Andalus exists simultaneously, it seems, in the land and in the poem.

I felt alone in language here, but also as a poet, someone who seeks always to see, and as a Muslim in a place with nearly a thousand years of history as a Muslim country that then quite brutally and systematically sought to eradicate that history while simultaneously appropriating the most commodifiable parts of it. "How does a place become / a reflection of its image in myth, / or an adjective of speech?" Darwish asks. "And is a thing's image stronger / than the thing itself?"[30]

This confused space between an actual place and the way the exile experiences place—both "there," the place he's left, and "here," the place he finds himself—is mirrored, for Darwish, in the multiple awarenesses of self within the individual. "If it weren't for my imagination / my other self would have told me: / You are not here!" he writes. It's imagination that serves Darwish the strongest as a way of being present anywhere, as a way of keeping the lost homeland alive and real. "You, O Self," he writes later, "are one of the adjectives of the place." The poet makes himself into a transformational conduit, able to bear the metaphor and the burden for sustaining the dream and desire of home: "As for me, I will enter the mulberry trees / where the silkworm makes me into a silk thread, / then I'll enter a woman's needle in / one of the myths / and fly like a shawl with the wind . . ."

Darwish left Beirut for Paris in 1982 with a stopover in Athens, Greece, where he met Yannis Ritsos. Years later, while in Chile at the house of Pablo Neruda, Darwish recalled the incident in "Like a Mysterious Incident." The distance of time—the poet recollecting a moment—is thus amplified by a second remove: Darwish is in Chile remembering his meeting with Ritsos in Athens, when the older poet embraced him and declared they were brothers:

> So I felt that I had won, and that I had been broken
> like a diamond, that nothing but light remained of me[31]

The condition of love is dual, of victory and of being broken, but also of being refined to pure light. The two poets share a conversation and "memories about the future." "My brother / in poem!" Darwish writes, "poetry has a bridge over / yesterday and tomorrow." He seeks to exist out of time, or rather in all times at once. In this way it will be possible for him to look forward to a history of returning home.

Ritsos himself is not satisfied with either the myth-making process of the exiles nor the idea of "exiting mythology." When Darwish asks what is poetry, Ritsos (the character in the poem Darwish himself is writing) replies, "It is the mysterious incident . . . is that inexplicable longing / that makes a thing into a specter, and / makes a specter into a thing." This transformative power of the written word enables Darwish to confront dual, triple, quadruple awarenesses and realities within his own individual self. This preoccupation with finding the other in his self—being constructed of more than one condition—seems tied to his loneliness and longing. "I am the child and the elderly," he writes, and "My exterior is my interior."

Darwish, once more, finds every possibility of liberation in art and imagination:

> Whenever my prison becomes narrow I spread into everything
> and my language widens as a pearl that lights up
> each time night is on patrol

Finally, he confesses to Ritsos how much he has learned from the older poet: "I learned / how to train myself to love / life and how to row in the white / Mediterranean looking for the way and for home or / for the duality of way of home." Ritsos is gruff and displeased; he doesn't respond, except to say, "Your Odysseus will come back safe, / he'll come back . . ."

The two men for a moment become poetic opposites—Ritsos fastened, silent and lonely, to one spot of geography, one house, alienated while life swirls around him, promising an eventual return from exile; Darwish cast into the wind of exile, spending decades moving from city to city, trying desperately to fix himself to a place that can only be found in language and the poem. At the close of "Like a Mysterious Incident," he once again invokes Neruda and his home on the Pacific coast, triangulating the moment of memory far from both Athens and Palestine, and imagines Ritsos, instead of promising the unlikely end to exile, "entering at that time / one of his myths, saying to one of his goddesses: / If there must be a journey, then let it be / an eternal one!"

Leaving Córdoba and the Mezquita behind, I traveled first to Toledo and then to Madrid. It was a jarring journey, because all traces of the Arab-fusion architecture disappeared. The aspects I considered most "Spanish" seemed gone, replaced instead by what seems to be more Central European/Austrian imperial architecture, in this odd city, founded by Arabs and named "Magerit." The last trace is a fragment of the old city wall from the ninth century, partitioned off just south of the cathedral. There's no plaque telling you what you're looking at, no preservation effort either.

The thing I keep noticing, of course, are the cities being built on top of each other—buildings from different times and cultures occupying the same physical space—streets with two or three names, all the various old cities, Barcelona, Valencia, Málaga, revealing beneath the modern streets the ancient Phoenician, Greek and Roman ruins. We think we don't have this coexistence of places in America, but we do. The serpent mound, all the destroyed holy places, the pueblo ruins—even Broadway is said to follow the ancient Indian path down the island.

Perhaps part of the American malaise, as Žižek suggests, is that we try to live out of the context of history, in our culture, in our architecture, in our monuments. Mount Rushmore, for example, is an attempt to literally inscribe American history onto the timeless landscape. It fails in its project because it is a fake place. It's enough to see the postcard or the image in the movies—those are the *real* Mount Rushmore for the vast majority of Americans who will never venture into the South Dakota mountains to look at the actual thing. The image and not the actual object is the culturally real thing, like the fallen Twin Towers, more icons for an abstract concept than actually compelling architecture when they were extant.

And if it is true that American political reality now marks the very stone of the continent, then the Córdoban caliphate was just as real, lasting from 756 C.E. until roughly 1031 C.E., decades longer than the current American government. Muslim nations on the Iberian peninsula existed from 711 until 1492, hundreds of years longer than the European presence in the Americas.

Of course you can't suppress history or pretend it didn't happen. The cathedral inside the Mezquita, though perhaps invisible in images, is necessarily part of the structure now, the way Peri Rossi's exile is permanent, the way Palestine and Israel are intimately a part of one another now, the way even now Arab Spain yet exists.

At the Museum of Contemporary Art in Barcelona, I saw an exhibit of Francesc Torres pictures on the forensic archeology of some of the unexcavated mass graves from the Spanish Civil War. The ground itself was scarred still. After the death of Franco, an unwritten agreement sprang up—there were no retributions, no reconciliation commissions—life just went on, nobody asked questions. It must have been like that also after the expulsion of the Jews and Muslims from Spain, their properties confiscated by the bankrupt monarchy to fund the exploration of the American continents.

But through silence, through the empty landscape, a city is a thing that cannot forget itself, but exists in all places at once. What is a city, after all, but an abstraction, non-representational, a concatenation of events through time and space? And what about our glum former assertion: that a city can only be made real once it has been left? That a country can only be known by its exiles? Jerusalem, Beirut, Sarajevo, Montevideo are all cities of desire, true, but all also actually exist. In Magritte's *La Clef des Champs,* the real field can only be seen once the image of it is shattered. An exile, myth maker extraordinaire, perhaps has no better shot at seeing the actual city than does a citizen.

As a collective enterprise, the city rotates in permanent un-fixity in its relationship with the individual observer. In some cases, the city itself acts out its violence—Lorca was taken from his house by a mob, taken and murdered by the city itself; there was no single actor, no one to take responsibility or blame. The collective murder passed into history with the close of the Franco era and the closing of the book on the acts of the past. Of course the murdered poet cannot be forgotten by his nation. He haunts it always, defines its very contours by the fact of his writing—language after all being a version of the fallen angel, language given as punishment for the building of Babel, but also perhaps as fulfilled prayer. There is a verse of the Quran which reads, "You asked us to make the spaces between you wider and so we scattered you with a terrible scattering."

For Etel Adnan, "Andalusia is the first loss, the death of the Mother, and of the orchards of which Lorca was the last tree."[32] In "Eleven Planets," Darwish's speaker, a poet who is going into exile, comforts himself with the thought that "my words of love will fall into Lorca's poems; he'll live on in my bedroom and see what I have seen of the Bedouin moon."[33] The kinship he feels—in the future tense—with the as-yet-to-come poet provides comfort for the tragedy of exile: "I am the Adam of the two

Edens, I who lost paradise twice / So expel me slowly, and kill me slowly, / under my olive tree, / along with Lorca . . ."

What you have is a locality of existence within perceptual form, a body with hopes of course of understanding the infinite. The thought of the body continues to be the way Darwish sees the poem and poetic form itself, highly formal, with intricate structures and metaphor that, as in a Sufi tradition, seem merely modes of harnessing ineffable energies. And so, usually, the poems do not end themselves with great flourishes or declarations, but rather with wild gestures, gesticulations into silence. One of my favorite of Darwish's devices is a coupling of a metaphysical idea with a quotidian physical reality. In "A Poetry Stanza / The Southerner's House," Darwish imagines himself standing with another poet who has died. He describes the scene, "Standing together . . . on eternity's bank . . . here is death's bicycle approaching."[34]

The other poet has transcended his death because, he says, "I didn't interfere with what the birds do to me / and with what the night carries / of passion's ailment." Darwish too wants to transcend place and the constraints of language, but most of all he yearns to transcend the stricture of self, transcend alienation and the barriers between objects and people. The other poet, the "southerner," as he calls him, "knows the path of vagabonds / like the back of his heart . . . No 'there' for him, / no 'here,' no address for the chaotic / no clothes rack for speech." In poetry one can fuse awareness, see into the past and the future at once, put an end to the loneliness of the soul. Though the southerner goes on to say, "I am my self's / radiant sound: I am he you and we are I," he also understands the requirements of putting a form to the emotions. He is "stern with his poem's form," and is a "brilliant / craftsman who saves meter from the roar of the storm."

But is it really possible for poetry to mend exile? "The land expands as much as your dream's measure," Darwish writes. "And the land is the mother of the bleeding imagination." It's a hopeless case, it seems, but still the only and best option. The dead poet says finally, "Take me to the house, / the house of the last metaphor . . . / for I am O stranger a stranger here / and nothing pleases me." Darwish, still wanting to find the answer for himself, presses him, "And what about the soul?" The poet has no answer for him, and the poem drifts off into silence: "It will sit near my life / for nothing proves me living / and nothing proves me dead / it will live, as it is / mystified and blue . . ."

At the end of the poem, a door, but a door unlabeled, a door that leads nowhere.

Mehmedinovic's cross-country journey is followed by a long sequence called "This Door Is Not an Exit." The sequence is obsessed with both physical/quotidian and metaphysical location, as in "I never had a house of my own," or "in the Maclean's parking lot." Throughout the sequence, though surrounded by people, he does not speak or otherwise interact with them physically. He sits beside them or sees them in photographs, but the one moment he is with another person interacting—folding sheets at a motel—he specifically eschews physical touch—in order to avoid the shock of static electricity. There are also plenty of poets in the sequence, but once again, not actually physically interacting with him: there's Gerard Malanga, his eyes closed, listening to Mehmedinovic read; there's a book by Darwish that Mehmedinovic himself is reading; and finally there's Czeslaw Milosz, outside whose apartment Mehmedinovic finds himself. Like Ritsos and his near-encounters through his last poems, Mehmedinovic does not encounter Milosz; the poem ends on the street, looking up the hill toward the apartment of the older poet.

There are two moments of curious contact within the sequence. In the first, an expert on bird calls teaches the poet that "the same kind of bird sings / Different songs in different places" and that he is trying to discover the "Kind of sorrow you feel away from home."[35] The poet confesses:

> I can't say I'm too happy about his gift
> . . . .
> Since I know nothing can reconcile the
> Sorrow of exile from the grief
>   of telling the dialects
> of southern Slavs apart

Because of the history of his own exile, the ability to actually and cleanly tell dialects apart—know who is a Croat or Bosnian or Serb, thus who is the enemy—is too much to bear; in fact, if the bird expert is right, the accents come from the same people; nations and even languages are mere fictions. It's heartbreaking knowledge.

In another poem about animals on the facing page, the poet spies from the street an animal that shouldn't be where it is—an African chimp pushing his body against the glass of a window on an apartment above. The poet experiences a surreal moment of unhinged reality: "I was sure I was already dead / and didn't know it // And that I'd gone over to the other side / Where borders between continents / don't exist."[36] Ironically, it's the American landscape, dotted by cities with the same name, strangely borderless, eerily homogenous, that holds the possibility for him of an escape from the disruptions of war.

Mehmedinovic never quite seems to adapt to the strangeness, never tastes the sweetness of exile as Peri Rossi begins to, or becomes able to spin it into the metaphor of itself as Darwish does. Like Ritsos's, his internal numbness seems matched, even comforted by the numbness of the suburban landscape of parking lots and motel rooms that surrounds him. When it comes to the question of returning, he writes, "I always answer differently." On the one hand, he says, "I can't really reconcile myself with getting old and the / Picture I have of myself looking for advice on americanheart.com," yet he confesses, "I am, in fact, where you are, to make / Your weariness inspire meaning." He ends the sequence with answerless geography, a fish market, the Potomac River, yachts in the marina.

And then, quite suddenly, he breaks with the poem form and turns to the inspiring source behind his sequence, a quote from Darwish: "I am an exile. / . . . Take me like a toy, a brick from the wall of your house / So our children will remember to return."[37] Like the key to the house in Toledo, Mehmedinovic is wondering what is left to him of the old nation if he has given up hope of returning, if everything is in fact exile. He recounts the story of his own son taking photographs of doors, never himself having had a permanent home either.

The photograph of the door, which inspired the poems, labeled "This door is a non-exit," is followed by a caption bearing slightly different wording: "This door is not an exit." Between the two wordings there is a little Möbius loop of affirmation of negativity and negation of positivity that perfectly fits the state of mind that inhabits the poems.

The final coda poem is dedicated to Ammiel Alcalay, the translator of the book. Mehmedinovic, standing outside Milosz's apartment, is reminded of Sarajevo. Originally, he writes, "I had wanted to show the symbols of Islam // In the light of so-called western metaphysics / And I wanted to renew the forgotten // Notion of Jesus . . . But it all ends in pure desire." In a move worthy of Darwish, he writes, "I feel like I'm ready, because // There's nothing else I want to posses."

In the gesture of interrupting his sequence to acknowledge Mahmoud Darwish as inspiration for the poem, and then to devote a poem to Alcalay as collaborator in bringing the poem to the citizens of the country in which it was written, Mehmedinovic enacts the same gesture of generosity and community that Darwish did with his poem on Ritsos, written in the house of Neruda. The moment of communion with Milosz, despite never meeting him, results in the final acceptance of the possibilities inherent in the position of the exiled.

This is the mind of loneliness. No one speaks back because no one can. And because no one can speak everyone must. Poems settle into sequences of thought rather than actual narrative because they cannot bear to be finished with themselves, to throw away the keys, to make of exile an actual home. As Mehmedinovic writes, "It seems we've come / a long way alone in sorrow only when / we're weary and its then the grave of every one of us is in Palestine."[38]

In a poem, this spatial and historical consciousness appears as layered consciousnesses of both a city and a person that can exist in all places in all times at once. Unlike Peri Rossi, who elected not to return and thus retained the feeling of her first exile, even to the point of questioning its reality, wondering if the condition of exile is internal and not external—"Did there ever once exist a city called Montevideo?"—Darwish never had a chance to "go back": Birweh is razed, the site doesn't exist anymore and the homeland, like mythical Al-Andalus, becomes idea as much as reality. As he writes in "Eleven Planets," "Death, be a blessing on the stranger who sees the unseen more clearly than the real . . . Where is the road to anything? I see the unseen more clearly than / a street that is no longer my street. Who am I after the night of the estranged?"[39]

I feel similarly unidentified and unidentifiable. Why did I come here to Europe, I asked myself in the ruined city of Madinat-a-Zahra, on the outskirts of Córdoba, to see ruins and remnants of the past? I had to doubly remind myself that it was not the European powers that ultimately destroyed the Córdoban caliphate, but the fundamentalist elements within the society itself. It was a Muslim army that stormed Madinat-a-Zahra and tore it brick from brick. If Al-Andalus, like Palestine for Mehmedinovic, has become a metaphor for the condition of exile, it's a quite complicated one.

And at any rate, at a certain moment in history, Jews and Muslims shared their exile. One wonders then, could it ever be possible, in the future, for villages not yet destroyed, to become that—not one thing constructed upon the destroyed ruins of another or one thing colonizing another in space like the minaret of Sevilla or the Mezquita-cathedral, but each thing culturally and physically present at once—Isaac and Ishmael both in the presence of their father at the same time, perhaps not arguing over who will receive the honor of having his throat cut?

That place, whether called Jerusalem, Al-Andalus, Sarajevo or Montevideo, is the future life of both nations and language.

NOTES

I am indebted to Maria Rosa Menocal, from whose book my historical information on Al-Andalus was drawn. Gratitude also to Ammiel Alcalay and Fady Joudah, who provided me with insight on their translations. On most occasions, I have used Marilyn Buck's translation of Peri Rossi. In the second and third quotations, I used lines translated by Marco Wilkinson.

1. Mahmoud Darwish, "Eleven Stars over Andalusia" in *The Veiled Suit,* by Agha Shahid Ali, trans. Agha Shahid Ali (New York: W. W. Norton & Company, 2009), 301.

2. Cristina Peri Rossi, *State of Exile,* trans. Marilyn Buck (San Francisco: City Lights Books, 2008), xxiii.

3. Ibid., 5.

4. Ibid., 103.

5. Dan Pagis, *Points of Departure,* trans. Stephen Mitchell (Philadelphia: Jewish Publication Society of America, 1981), 23.

6. Darwish, "Eleven Stars over Andalusia," 302.

7. Rossi, *State of Exile,* xxiii.

8. Ibid., 91.

9. Ibid., 93.

10. Ibid., 145.

11. Ibid., 107.

12. Ibid., 109.

13. Yannis Ritsos, *Late into the Night,* trans. Martin McKinsey (Oberlin, OH: Oberlin College Press, 1995), 26.

14. Darwish, "Eleven Stars over Andalusia," 309.

15. Ritsos, *Late into the Night,* 31.

16. Ibid., 55.

17. Ibid., 36.

18. Semezdin Mehmedinovic, *Nine Alexandrias,* trans. Ammiel Alcalay (San Francisco: City Lights Books, 2002), 3.

19. Andrew Buncombe, "Bush Rejects Taliban Offer to Surrender bin Laden," *Independent,* October 15, 2001.

20. Etel Adnan, *In the Heart of the Heart of Another Country* (San Francisco: City Lights Books, 2005), xii.

21. Darwish, "Eleven Stars over Andalusia," 305.

22. Mehmedinovic, *Nine Alexandrias,* 16.

23. Ibid., 29.

24. Ibid., 15.

25. Mahmoud Darwish, "With the Mist So Dense on the Bridge," trans. Mohammad Shaheen and Amro Naddy, *Virginia Quarterly Review* (Summer 2008).

26. Maria Rosa Menocal, *The Ornament of the World* (New York: Little, Brown and Company, 2002), 249.

27. Rossi, *State of Exile,* xxxv.

28. Mahmoud Darwish, *Memory for Forgetfulness,* trans. Ibrahim Muhawi (Berkeley: University of California Press, 1995), 6–22.

29. Mahmoud Darwish, *The Butterfly's Burden,* trans. Fady Joudah (Port Townsend, WA: Copper Canyon Press, 2007), 291.

30. Ibid., 293.

31. Ibid., 307.

32. Etel Adnan, *Of Cities and Women* (Sausalito, CA: Post-Apollo Press, 1993), 56.

33. Darwish, "Eleven Stars over Andalusia," 303.
34. Darwish, *Butterfly's Burden,* 299.
35. Mehmedinovic, *Nine Alexandrias,* 46.
36. Ibid., 47.
37. Ibid., 53.
38. Ibid., 40.
39. Darwish, "Eleven Stars over Andalusia," 307.

A Brief Poetics

To Layla Al-Attar

The first language of poetry I heard was the language of prayer, my father reciting from the Quran and other scripture. Part of poetry will always, for me, have the rhythms of those long lines, the structure of those couplets, the second line answering the first in some way, usually not merely narrative; also the strangeness of a language I do not understand, clotted with consonants that do not exist in English, modulated by vowels that English-speaking throats can rarely manage. And of course, profoundly, poetry for me is the voice of another, reciting to me, to an audience that sometimes recites along.

I wrote myself together in time not to know something but to sketch something that was fleeting, and more often than not I wouldn't know—I'd come to the last line of a poem and not understand what to write there and leave it blank, or leave it with a placeholder. It took time and an unfolding life to understand what I might be getting at or really what might be getting at me.

A blank page has a life in it of course, any poet will tell you that, or a cloud in it, as Thich Nhat Hanh wrote: "you could see it, if only you were a poet."[1]

It's not that I think poetry is strange or removed from actual life—it's that we are. It's us who are swirled into strangeness—eating synthetic fruit, drinking cola that is not cola, obsessed with reality television, the supreme achievement of our fantasy life: directed, edited, performed "reality." What do you do in such a life when someone suddenly speaks in tongues?

Motivated mostly by alienation, rage and yes, stupidity, the war is on, and what do you say to it? Layla Al-Attar, one of the premier artists of the Arab world, was also the director of the national center for art in Baghdad. She was a leading voice against the U.S. bombing missions against Iraqi military targets that continued long after the Gulf War ended in 1991; with great frequency these missiles were killing civilians, often far astray of their military targets. On the morning of June 27, 1993, President Bill Clinton ordered a strike of twenty-three Tomahawk missiles against various strategic targets. Seven of these went astray of their intended military targets and landed in residential areas of Baghdad.

How do we even tell of actual things in the world? When they are so horrific we can barely actually imagine them? You should write the last line of this story yourself.

Language that finishes itself in the mind requires the reader to be a community in participation with the writer and the text of the poem itself. When I try to construct a narrative, it interrupts itself; when I try to write pure lyric, story appears, tendrils of plants growing through the pavement. On the fortieth day many things happen—throughout spiritual traditions and religions of the world, forty days is a period of spiritual charging and release. On the fortieth day you are most filled, quivering almost, not knowing what happens next, but certainly about to happen.

To me the most exciting thing that happens in a poem is this reach—of the writer in the direction of the ineffable but with the fervent prayer of reaching some place, a hapless supplicant who flings himself at the flat, black sky, but hoping for heaven. The reader might come to a text in this same way, ready to leap somewhere, blessed to be in the presence of human experience.

Because Clinton wished to "minimize possible deaths of innocent civilians," the missiles were launched in the dead of the night.[2] Was she awake, busy preparing for the planned major exhibition of her work? Or sleeping, warm and hovering in that place in between the dream-life and this one? What does it sound like approaching, and did the windows shatter inwards or outwards?

Layla Al-Attar's death is the new moon in the sky of your historical consciousness—new moon because you didn't know it was there. Occluded and untold, it disappeared in the drift of events at the end of the last century, but though unilluminated in the American perception of the world, it existed, exerting a gravitational pull nonetheless. Imagine it—there are countless events just like it, millions of narratives not untangling themselves as in the Western perception of fate—the Three Fates, kindly separating and measuring every life—but rather perhaps closer to the Islamic notion of kismet, an incredibly complex interconnected network of links between every living being throughout all time.

We have to learn how to look in myriad directions at once and to simultaneously understand the countless ways in which we cannot see. Death extinguished the life of a brilliant artist and destroyed hundreds of her paintings. We cannot measure the loss—it is more horrific than can be told in standard prose—it requires a grammar, vocabulary and shape quite beyond. In science fiction time-travel stories, the horror of death is told in future time—someone changes their own past, and all sorts of people begin blinking out of existence, futures that don't happen.

The future changes the past of course. The poem, the writer, the reader and the existing life are not fixed points in time and space. If war is a failure of the imagination, then poets and poetry will have something to say about it. But I think we should remember that the death of Layla Al-Attar was bought and paid for by our labor, our tax dollars, our support of U.S. foreign policy. Al-Attar was a civilian, killed in peacetime.

Perhaps there was a future in which Layla Al-Attar lived; she wasn't home when the missile struck, or the missiles were never launched, perhaps the missiles were never constructed. I dreamed it without knowing it. Hovering between sleep and dream and waking life, I look everywhere for that text, wanting to wage preemptive peace by sky-writing it above all the capitals of the world, wanting to recite it to the heavens, recite it to you.

NOTES

1. Thich Nhat Hanh, *The Heart of Understanding* (Berkeley: Parallax Press, 1988), 3.

2. David Von Drehle and R. Jeffrey Smith, "U.S. Strikes Iraq for Plot to Kill Bush," *Washington Post,* June 27, 1993.

3

Poetry and Silence

When one speaks, who answers back? What is a question in a poem? Sometimes I think there should be no answer—not that silence is the answer, but the gesture of the question is the point.

God's silence ceases to be troubling—spiritually or politically—if one views wondering this way. It's not reassuring. It's a changing of the usual "Why is God silent?" to "There is a God who is silent—now what?"

Here's one of the poems, titled "Joe the Lion II," from Cynthia Cruz's *Ruin:*

Then, the great machinery begins.
The last time anybody saw you, the fawn
Walked into the field, the edge
Of night coming on like so many black wings.

Saint Francis, when he broke the wolf,
Leaned into the stinking sea of wine and blood that was
That animal's body. I am
The wolf. God is the night

I must not creep into.

Into this, then, the world:

I ask for a ship
And then, no ship comes.[1]

At the Folger Library in early 2006, Katie Ford, Eve Grubin and I did a reading together called "Young Poets and Faith," followed by a discussion with the audience. During the discussion period, I spoke about my preference for confusion and doubt as a way of approaching spiritual questions—that once we fell back on the paragraphs of received wisdom we ceased to be engaged.

In the Quran, after a cryptic story or pronouncement, you often find the verse, "Surely there are signs in this for those of you who reflect." It's my favorite verse, not because I am naturally contrary and want to believe the opposite of what the commentators or religious establishment declares—though there is that—but more because it is the book's invitation to me to try to make sense out of my life, to reconcile the material facts of my life with spiritual values.

When I spoke at the Folger about the idea that there are revelations everywhere, that the sky speaks, stones speak, that there is no silence of God, a speaker from the audience challenged me by reminding me that it is this kind of thinking that has gotten us into a lot of trouble. People who believe they understand what the sky or the stones or God is saying can make a lot of trouble for everyone else. Especially if there is more than one group who believes they have heard it, and they have heard different things.

To me it is beautiful that God could speak out of both sides of his Mouth. It makes perfect sense that different kinds of people would require different kinds of religion. Yoga makes allowances for this—certain people do hatha practice (of which the postures—*asana* and breathing—*pranayama*—are a part); others practice bhakhti or jnana or karma yoga. They are all valid spiritual paths.

As Vivekananda and Hafez both wrote (and my grandfather Sajjad Sayeed was fond of quoting), "All rivers go into the ocean."

Being at an empty beach, looking at the end of the world, listening to the roaring in and out of the waters, is a version of silence, answerless silence.

As I think about my own ideas about poetry and art, I notice how often I have swerved away from actual content—in either poetry, music, painting or dance—and toward the idea of "silence": Rothko's monochrome fields, Martin's white paintings, Chandra's drones, the stillness of *butoh*. In poetry, I lean toward the small, the fraught, the nearly silent.

So once again I ask myself, is it just because I don't want to be shown things? That I prefer art to be an empty mirror—just pure potential energy to let me fill with whatever occupies me emotionally at the moment?

Is art merely that—a gateway through to the divine or to happiness or whatever is on the other side?

In the rehearsals for our dance performance of "Dancing on Water," Susan Osberg worked with all the various dancers individually, and not until the first full dress rehearsal, the week before the show opened, did she stitch all the pieces together. It was an exciting and dynamic moment to witness the full canvas we had each individually been creating.

Though I have thought that dance differs from poetry in that it depends on being seen, the night I performed my part—the dance and recitation of poems—I was left in darkness, lights shining on me from every direction. I could see no one, hear no one. I was very much alone there, on the stage, declaiming to darkness.

If prayer is like this, then poetry—and this writing—is also like this. In loneliness we wonder about human connection, what happens when or if someone will read a poem. This is the central drama of Lucille Clifton's poetic sequence "brothers," in which Lucifer speaks seven times to God, each time waiting for—and not hearing—God's answer. Louise Glück's book-length sequence *The Wild Iris* likewise presents a gardener who believes she is not heard by God, and in turn is hearing neither God nor the flowers of her garden, both of which are speaking.

Here lies the difference between what I was talking about the Folger Library and what my respondent was saying. In one sequence, the speaker comes to accept that silence of God as part of God; in the other the speaker never stops looking for signs, but is never able to see.

As Geri Doran writes in "Beyond the 45th Parallel," from her book *Resin:*

> Like alchemy, endlessness is a fiction.
> We are always halfway to somewhere.
> I want more than transmutation:
> I want the god I pray to to be real.[2]

In the dance I empty myself first and concentrate on the brown earth. Then slowly as I breathe, I visualize sky blue streaming into me and filling me; then my arms slowly rise as wings. There is a mystical process in the physical dance.

If a tree falls in the forest.

Partially it is what lies beneath the surface or what threatens to break free that is engaging. An art that has had previous lives or perhaps future lives is radioactive, always on the verge of becoming something else in the hands or eyes or ears of a real recipient. The idea that we might know fully what we are doing means there might be something more at work. In an Agnes Martin painting it is the space between her carefully sketched lines and the anarchy of the surface, a quiet anarchy. In Chandra, it is the universe that is to be found in a single tone.

As far as true spiritual music goes, de-centered and reflective in all the ways I have spoken about, Alice Coltrane comes closer than anything I've heard. I love myself and lose myself in the visceral immediate sound of Coltrane's insistent movements against the subtle and eternal wash of the background sounds. Coltrane is a yogi and a swami—is this music supposed to be a literal depiction of the individual spirit against the Divine?

Eve, Katie and I had read once before at a similar event, this one organized by the Auburn Theological Seminary in New York City. We were each to read work that we felt was spiritually inflected or dealt with God and religion, and then there was to be a discussion with the students following the event. It was Eve's first reading after the publication of her first book of poetry, *Morning Prayer*. She read several poems in keeping with the theme of the evening and then apologized, saying, "This next poem has nothing to do with God, but I would like to read it anyway." Upon conclusion of the very beautiful poem, there was a moment of silence, and then the rabbi sitting next me called out, "But that poem is completely about God!"

Here's "Nineteenth Century Novel II" by Eve Grubin:

> I am the heroine
> in a novel, and there are twenty pages left.
> Someone is reading the novel, holding
> the numbered pages in their hands, almost finished.

Every night, in bed, they read my story
with the novel propped up on their chest.
I want them to read quickly, but they read
a page a night, without
urgency, as if there is no rush
before turning off the light.

I read the scriptures. Instead of reciting back to them the prescribed answers, I wrote my letter on twelve pages from the sky and folded it into little boats to float away on the stream at midnight.

There was no answer.

Somewhere now, between map and maelstrom, I am getting ready to write back.

NOTES

1. Cynthia Cruz, *Ruin* (Farmington, MA: Alice James Books, 2006), 42.

2. Geri Doran, *Resin* (Baton Rouge, LA: Louisiana State University Press, 2005), 23.

adam and his mother

Lucille Clifton's Prosodic Line

Lucille Clifton is known as a poet of simple and clear diction, informed by trickster sensibility, and is as facile with the cadences of King James as she is with Black vernacular. Though she is often seen as a prophet-figure taking Blakean dictation, her poems are marked not only by spiritual gravity but by the humbler attentions of a working poet utilizing the various tools of poetic craft. Clifton has often discussed her roots as a poet in poetic form. Her mother, Thelma, used to write poetry in iambic pentameter and would go so far as to criticize young Lucille's poetic attempts (in free verse), saying, "Oh honey, that ain't a poem."[1] Clifton also cites Yeats, Conrad Aiken and Sonia Sanchez—another poet who marries colloquial oral speech to received form and poetic meters—as influences.

Clifton regularly uses elements of metrical rhythm in all of her poems—but she more frequently shifts meter line by line, usually for oral or performative effect. Clifton, taking a cue from Sonia Sanchez, sometimes uses the traditionally enjambed free verse line to great effect in this way. If you read a straight sentence through, the poem will sound truly like free verse, but if you read with slight caesurae at the end of each line, the rhythmic modulation can be clearly heard. For example, her poem "moses":

moses

i walk on bones
snakes twisting
in my hand
locusts breaking my mouth

> an old man
> leaving slavery
> home is burning in me
> like a bush
> God got his eye on[2]

Each line functions as a different poetic phrase, and each has its own meter, the first line iambic, the second a heavy stress-trochee pair, the third anapestic, the fourth line starting in trochees and ending in an iamb—the rhythmic switch emphasizes the actual "breaking" going on—and the fifth line with a light stress followed by a spondee. Moses's human self and his human elements—his action walking, his hand, his mouth—are all iambic, small and delicate against the trochaic and elemental twisting, the locusts, slavery itself.

After a trochee-dactyl line and a trochaic line, the penultimate anapest leads into one of Clifton's favorite poetic strategies—heavy stresses, in this case a spondee, then a light stress ("his") followed by a second spondee. The interruptions of the line breaks force the ear away from hearing any regular pattern in the rhythm and heightens the music of the interruptive incantation, which puts Moses's human qualities in opposition to the immense forces of nature and God around him. He's once again iambic when he compares home to the burning bush before driving home the final line of the poem—God isn't the burning bush in this version of the myth, but its observer. Merely by watching something, God causes it to flower, so too with creation, so too with Moses himself.

Clifton often uses a switch from trochaic intonation to a brief iambic energy build-up before deploying a series of heavy stresses that declaim with biblical fervency. This switch in meter brings emphasis through the sentence and allows the heavy stresses—sometimes as many as six in a row—to do their rhythmic work. Even when she provides the interlude of a light stress, as in "moses," she remains more or less symmetrical and musical in her use of the heavy stresses.

Like Sonia Sanchez, one of her acknowledged influences, Clifton often deploys the sentence *against* the line to heighten a sense of drama or difficulty. Sanchez's poem "Personal Letter

No. 2" is a good example of the line breaks themselves torquing the emotional content of the poem. In this first incorrect version of the poem, Sanchez's lines are re-assembled, and the punctuation is regularized:

> i speak skimpily to you about apartments i no longer dwell in
> and children who chant their disobedience in choruses.
> if i were young i would stretch you with my wild words
> while our nights run soft with hands, but i am what i am:
> woman, alone amid all this noise.[3]

But here's Sanchez's actual poem, with irregular punctuation and very strategic line breaks that interrupt and intrude on normal conversational rhythms of speech:

> i speak skimpily to
> you about apartments i
> no longer dwell in
> and children who
> chant their dis
> obedience in choruses.
> if i were young
> i wd stretch you
> with my wild words
> while our nights
> run soft with hands.
> but i am what i
> am. woman. alone
> amid all this noise.

Lines continually end with personal referents ("i," "who," "you"), suspending the action. In one dramatic case an actual word is broken without hyphenation, and another, "would," is compressed into the near gnomic "wd." It's the penultimate line, however—"am. woman. alone"—that essentializes the drama and demonstrates most clearly how Sanchez is able to position the brokenness of the sentences against the poetic line to represent the sense of loss and alienation felt by the speaker. As in the Clifton poem, Sanchez closes the piece with a heavy-stress-packed line—double iambs (including "alone" from the previous line) followed by three heavy stresses.

Clifton uses this scheme of sentences of various and irregular lengths coupled with mid-sentence line breaks. Since a traditional use of meter—that is, regularly recurring metrical pattern—is clearly not her strategy, one must listen to the stresses line by line in order to detect patterns in the poem as a whole.

The first line of Clifton's "sarah's promise" has a strange but obvious rhythm: heavy-light-light-heavy, followed by the same pattern again: heavy-light-light-heavy: "who understands better than i," creating a brief caesura in the middle of the phrase. The heavy stress of the final "i" sounds iambic to the ear with the beginning of the following line—"the hunger in old bones"—but that line quickly transitions from iambs into the spondaic "old bones," finishing with the anapest at the beginning of the third line, "for a son?" Clifton's speaker discursively announces "so here we are"—and the couple is presented in different meters: Abraham is metric (a dactyl-anapest pair creating, like her trochee-iamb switches, a little more rhythmic momentum in the phrase), and Sarah is all stress—three heavy stresses next to one another, framed by light stresses, an inverse of the first line of the poem: "abraham with his faith / and i my fury."

sarah's promise

who understands better than i
the hunger in old bones
for a son? so here we are,
abraham with his faith
and i my fury. jehovah,
i march into the thicket
of your need and promise you
the children of young women,
yours for a thousand years.
their faith will send them to you,
docile as abraham. now,
speak to my husband.
spare me my one good boy.[4]

The following sentence, spanning five lines of the poem, is full of stresses, but the pattern, due to Clifton's interruptive feet, keeps switching, sounding trochaic and iambic by turn. Listen

to this fake and metrically more regular version of the line to
see how tenuously the original refuses regularity:

> jehovah, i march
> to the thicket of need
> and promise you
> children of women for
> a thousand years . . .

Instead the small interruptions disrupt the ear and force the passage into a more conversational tone. At one point a clot of heavy
stresses—"young women, / yours"—once again foregrounds a
regularity of rhythm and leads into a fourth, shorter iambic sentence that ends with the double dactyl "docile as abraham." The
final brief sentences are set apart from the rest of the poem by
the injunction "now" but sonically echo the longer sentences
with their dactyls "speak to my" and "spare me my." Clifton drives
home her point and returns her poem not to Abraham's rhythmic docility but to Sarah's anti-rhythmic fury with a final chain of
three heavy stresses next to one another:

> speak to my husband.
> spare me my one good boy.

In "monticello," an epigrammatic piece about the suspiciously
red-haired children of Sally Hemings, a woman enslaved on
Thomas Jefferson's estate, Clifton deploys three different meters
across four short lines:

> *monticello*
>
> God declares no independence.
> here come sons
> from this black sally
> branded with jefferson hair.[5]

The first line of the poem, a complete sentence, begins with a
heavy stress and ends in trochees, thus giving it a trochaic feel.
Because of the switch in stresses there are three heavy stresses
together in the middle of the line, making brief caesurae on

either side of the word "no," offering the denial extra emphasis: "God declares no independence." This is immediately
followed by two brief lines packed with six heavy stresses—a
line of declaration against the dominant historical narrative:
"here come sons / from this black sally." The first of these has
three heavy stresses in a row while the second, with its framing
of light stresses at the beginning and end of the line, seems to
draw the ear and the eye to the word "black" and to Sally herself at the end of the line.

These symmetrically stressed lines are released into the
rhythmic levity of the final line, a double dactyl followed by a
heavy stress, giving the end a light iambic sound: "branded with
jefferson hair." While it's true that ordinarily a heavy stress at
the end of regular meter (an iambic line in "moses," dactyls in
"sarah's promise") usually signifies gravity in Clifton's work,
here it has a more folksy and humorous sound, like Mother
Goose's famous double-dactyl heavy-stress line "hickory, dick-
ory, dock." The final line of "monticello," with its rhythmic
switch, seems to leaven the mood of the poem, making it a little
bit more witty, even jocular in tone, rather than the more
solemn declamatory tone of the second and third lines.

Although Clifton infrequently works in received forms, in
her recent collection *Mercy* she does includes a senryu, a Japanese form that deals with human emotions rather than subli-
mating observance into nature imagery the way haiku does.
Senryu are frequently darkly witty, while traditional haiku traffic
more in an earnest and wistful tone. Clifton's poem is called
"sonku," likely a play on Sonia Sanchez's adaptation of the senryu, called by Sanchez "songku" for their focus on rhythm and
music in addition to the bare observation that Japanese forms
are well known for.

sonku

his heart, they said was
three times the regular size.
yes, I said, I know.[6]

Once again, in a very short poem—the space of seventeen syllables, as a matter of fact—Clifton switches poetic meters in

each of the three lines. The very first phrase is an iamb, followed by a caesura and then another iamb with an extra syllable "was" at the end, leading into the second line and disallowing the kind of "inter-line" caesura that the rhythm of "moses" was so dependent on. This line is followed by Clifton's characteristic spondee and then an iamb-anapest pair that nonetheless has a little bit of a trochaic sound to it—specifically in "times the regular"—another example of the way Clifton's use of meter sometimes forces the sound of the line to an in-between action. The final line, iambs set up by an injunction (like Sarah's "now"), thuds with the sound of the dead man's heartbeat and the image's painful double entendre: "yes, i said, i know."

Many of Clifton's poetic strategies converge in her masterful poem "what did she know, when did she know it." The poem begins with a single-phrase line, but this is quickly disrupted by the second line, which contains not only an inverted verb but also a disrupted syntax of the declarative: "what it was the soft tap tap." This move from inquisitive to declarative is highlighted by the rhythmic shift to three heavy stresses in a row of "soft tap tap," which is echoed a few lines later in "sheet arced off":

> in the evenings
> what it was the soft tap tap
> into the room   the cold curve
> of the sheet arced off
> the fingers sliding in
> and the hard clench against the wall
> before and after[7]

Though the third line follows the tap grammatically "into the room," it is further disrupted by a mid-line (and visual) caesura before yet another set of heavy stresses in "cold curve." The poem then returns to lines that are nearly iambic single phrases (with the sole and disturbing interruption of "hard clench"), but is unable to sustain this cool approach in light of the difficult subject matter and soon dissolves into fracture and fragment, a pyrrhic foot (two light stresses) followed by a spondee, a caesura and another spondee and then a return to the tentative inquisitive:

> all the cold air   cold edges
> why the little girl never smiled

The irony here is that the question ("Why did the little girl never smile?") was not asked in her actual life, nor does it manage to articulate itself in the poem. It's also a line that drops its initial trochees into the dark caesura between "girl" and the first syllable of "never," enabling once again an iambic sound from "never" into "smiled." Clifton immediately switches in the final lines of the poem to a more painful interrogation—because everyone by this point has realized "why the little girl never smiled." Though intimated as a question, it serves to point out to the reader that there is something no one is talking about but that everyone (most pointedly here the mother) knows.

The two final questions are similarly asked without the normative punctuation of a question mark, perhaps symbolic of the fact that these are questions asked of a woman no longer alive, questions that skim the rawest surface of the child-as-adult's anger, questions that will never be answered:

> they are supposed to know everything
> our mothers   what did she know
> when did she know it

This poem continually switches between declarative and inquisitive, but the switch is not accompanied by either the punctuation or the normal grammatical constructions that would enable the reader to be accustomed to the new rhetorical mode. As a result it more closely imitates the mental structure of a child who does not understand the causal relationships, unable to understand why the father is acting against her in such a way, unable to understand why the mother does nothing, acts like she knows nothing. It's the chilling realization of the adult Clifton—that whether or not her mother knew of her abuse, each option is equally painful: "they are supposed to know everything / our mothers"—that drives the inquiry in the final lines of the poem:

what did she know, when did she know it

in the evenings
what it was the soft tap tap
into the room   the cold curve
of the sheet arced off
the fingers sliding in
and the hard clench against the wall
before and after
all the cold air   cold edges
why the little girl never smiled
they are supposed to know everything
our mothers   what did she know
when did she know it

Clifton's poems are to be read on the page and aloud. Her use of prosody and metrical elements, sustained and strategic, is sometimes counterintuitive and requires a more careful and engaged ear than listening to the rhythms in a poet more obviously trafficking in regular meter—to give two very opposite examples, someone like James Merrill or Susan Howe. In Clifton, meter is all strategy, switching within the poem to create added tension, suspension, humor or emphasis. She is as at home with a conversational tone as she is with those disconcerting trochee-iamb and dactyl-anapest switches. Paying attention to sound patterns in Clifton's lines, as well as the architecture of sound in the poems themselves, will greatly enrich understanding of her work's content and increase the aural pleasure of its music.

NOTES

1. Lucille Clifton, *Good Woman: Poems and a Memoir, 1969–1980* (Brockport, NY: BOA Editions, 1987), 160.

2. Ibid., 93.

3. Sonia Sanchez, *Shake Loose My Skin* (Boston: Beacon Press, 1999), 8.

4. Lucille Clifton, *The Book of Light* (Port Townsend, WA: Copper Canyon Press, 1993), 56.

5. Clifton, *Good Woman,* 126.

6. Lucille Clifton, *Mercy* (Rochester, NY: BOA Editions, 2004), 18.

7. Lucille Clifton, *The Terrible Stories* (Brockport, NY: BOA Editions, 1996), 52.

illuminate she could

Lucille Clifton's Lucifer

In Lucille Clifton's earlier work "Tree of Life," from her book *Quilting*, Adam and Eve speak about their experiences in the garden. It's interesting that neither attempts a prayer or address to God Himself. At the end of the sequence, Lucifer rises up to speak to us, a brief address, not an apology but an explanation:

> i the only lucifer
> light-bringer
> created out of fire
> illuminate i could
> and so
> illuminate i did."[1]

Lucille Clifton's imagination of Lucifer and God is radical for more than one reason. Rather than only Lucifer being the "adversary," both are imagined as stubborn old "brothers," equals in some understanding, part of each other somehow, though it is Lucifer who is in the position of supplicant, the younger brother perhaps, cast out of Heaven, excluded from God's company. Interestingly—and this is in line with a Sufi interpretation of Lucifer's exile, one Milton was also apparently familiar with—Clifton's Lucifer is not "satan" or "devil" precisely, but rather, as his name implies, a "light-bringer." This Lucifer still believes himself—perhaps his ongoing sin—to be superior to God, but for the most interesting of reasons—that God commanded him to bow to Adam, and he refused. Though punished, he maintains his innocence: "You commanded me to bow before no one but you and so I am more faithful than You are."

The poem proceeds, in eight short sections, to tell the story of Lucifer's initial attempt at reconciliation, indictment, declaration of superiority, half-hearted accusatory defense, matter-of-fact ignoring, condemnation, resignation and ultimately reconciliation with the Divinely reticent God. God, predictably, for His own unspoken reasons, does not or will not answer.

Clifton's Lucifer begins with an invitation—"come coil with me / here in creation's bed / among the twigs and ribbons of the past"—to reflection and discourse. Further, this Lucifer, as also evidenced by the title of the piece, has a certain view of his relationship to God. He imagines that God, like himself, is not quite omniscient in a traditional sense, but would be willing to rest with Lucifer, "like two old brothers / who watched it happen and wondered / what it meant."

Significantly, when Lucifer refers to himself and God together, the pronouns ("we," "us") are lowercase, but when he addresses God alone the pronouns are uppercase. It is likely the single instance in all of Clifton's work where a word is uppercase, since traditionally she eschews it in all instances, including proper names and the beginning of sentences. Somehow God becomes even more lonely and distant and distinct from this not-all-together pleasant mark of respect. Indeed, when Lucifer is not answered, he grows a little tart, saying to God, "You are beyond / even Your own understanding." We've moved past the mainstream ideas about divinity and individuality into a realm where it is possible not only for the divine to misunderstand humankind, but indeed to misunderstand itself. In fact, Lucifer attempts to explain to God that the very notion of human failing—"both he and she, / the odd ambition, the desire / to reach beyond the stars / ... / the loneliness, the perfect / imperfection"—is an essential part of God Himself.

The issue of creation's separation from Creator is one at the heart of spiritual practice and belief. In mainstream Judeo-Christian-Islamic traditions, there is a defined duality between the individual and the divine, and the ultimate goal of spiritual practice is for the individual to be admitted back into the company of the Divine. But in every religious tradition—from Christian to Hindu to Muslim to Jewish—there is another, nondualist view that holds that the individual is a broken-off part of the divine and yearns for a reunion with that Spirit.

It is funny to read Sufi poets, Christian mystics, New Age hippies and aged yogis all saying the same thing about God, but they do. Here one talks to God because of the mere existence of God, not because one is afraid of one extreme or in love with the other. After all, Lucifer is a fallen angel, once a part of God's inner circle. In the Sufi view, Lucifer has a critical role to play in Creation—by presenting humans with obstacles to God, he offers them an opportunity for a deeper and closer relationship than would be possible without any obstacles at all.

Even if he's considered merely a metaphor for the separation of the individual spirit from the Universal Spirit, one has to admit, if anyone's got a right to be testy with God, it's Lucifer. In fact, as many of the yogic texts argue, the individual spirit has got to get through the argument with God to get anywhere in terms of spiritual growth.

In his work *Self-Unfoldment,* Swami Chinmayananda writes of the individual spirit's journey inward through awareness of the body and physical existence, then through the "mind"—the sense-making and perceiving organ—to the intellect, a steadier awareness of existence. Through the intellect the self finds what's called the "bliss sheathe." You might expect that a union with God would happen in such a place, but in fact, it's there that a person confronts *maya*—the ultimate illusions of which the world is constructed. It plays out in science fiction all the time: heroes get to the ultimate inner sanctum in their quest for the "truth" and find nothing there but lies—Dorothy meets the actual Wizard; Neo confronts the Architect and learns the sorry truth about himself; Saladin Chamcha in *The Satanic Verses,* at the height of his transformation into a devil, finally gives into his rages and hatred and wakes up human.

The individual self, separated from God, left in a lonely world, ultimately has to face up to that silence. At first Lucifer declares the distinctiveness his separation has offered him, saying he is "blessed with / the one gift you cherish; / to feel the living move in me." Significantly, when Lucifer talks of Eve's creation, he refers to "the breast of Yourself / separated out and made to bear," but when he talks of his actual superiority to the unchanging God, the typography drops from upper- to lowercase.

Lucifer is clear about the fact that he is equal to Adam and Eve in the expulsion from the garden, which implies that for him, as for them, there is a possibility of redemption. His expulsion was not, he insists earlier in "tree of life," due to his own selfishness or desire for others to share his exile. In fact, Clifton suggests something more radical in section 4 of "brothers," called "in my own defense": "what could I choose," Lucifer asks, "but to slide along behind them, / they whose only sin / was being their father's children?" Clifton implies here that Lucifer *chose* his exile—further implying Adam and Eve's choice in their own exile—the true "sin" being the exercise of free will. In Clifton's cosmology not only does the temptation of Eve seem to be part of the whole plan, but Adam and Eve are also raised in status to being actual children of an again lowercase god.

Lucifer blames God here for not calling out to his children, but says further, "only in their fever / could they have failed to hear." It is an odd construction, because even though Lucifer has just accused God of not speaking, the grammar of the second clause implies he did call out, but the humans did not hear him. It is possible that it is God's silence that the humans cannot yet read. At any rate, given a choice between the fallen humans and the divine and silent God, Lucifer seems to know which side his bread is buttered on—that only through the experience of separation can he truly experience union—and exits the garden.

In the new world, the fallen Lucifer here never makes his transformation into Satan, he of the red skin and cloven hooves, horns protruding from his head. Clifton's Lucifer remains entranced with pleasure, the "vale of sheet and sweat after love," but at the same time recognizes all of it as "the outer world." Even though he meditates here on "delight," the poem ends with his grim foreshadowing of the end of it, "the bruising of his heel, my head, / and so forth." It's by engaging with the materials of the world, the pleasures of being alive, sex, the passing of time, "the sweet puff / of bread baking," that Lucifer is able to finally face up to his anger, the elemental anger that lies at the heart of dualistic belief: why does God allow suffering?

The failure in logic of dualistic philosophy goes like this: If there is an omnipotent God, then how can horrifying things—the death of a child, genocide, rape, the subversion of democratic governments for the sake of capital—be permitted to happen? What is the power of prayer then to alter the course of human actions? The power of positive thinking and a belief in saints not withstanding, excruciating brutality does visit itself upon otherwise innocent people. Lucifer's assault on the very nature of God, in section 6 of "brothers," is scathingly titled "the silence of God is God," a quote from Carolyn Forché. Lucifer means it sarcastically, and the section is distinct among the series for being one long sentence, adding to its rant-like qualities. Also, oddly, no question mark is used though the sentence is in fact a question, arriving at its final clause thus: "tell us why / You watched the excommunication of / that world and You said nothing." Clifton is nothing if not exact with her punctuation—questions marks have been used throughout the poems preceding this one—so it is almost as if, though he is in full-blown accusatory mode, Lucifer at last understands that God is not going to answer him. Perhaps it is that knowledge that allows him to finally touch the depth of his despair—a despair that every individual, perhaps particularly in the current moment, might feel. But perhaps deeper than that, Lucifer understands now that the dualistic language of questions and answers, the concept of God needing to justify Creation, is part of the separation, part of the exile itself.

Of "brothers," Hillary Holladay writes, "God's ambiguous silence puts the onus of speech on everybody else."[2] Lucifer is not—will never be—given answers of any kind. It occurs to him, somehow, that the very fact of his existence, not just having fallen, but actually having been able to fall, is a form of grace. His split tongue that manages to both adore and decry his absent brother is a form of proof somehow. He also comes to terms with his role and his relationship to his brother, rejoicing that he will be able to "curl one day safe and still / beside You / at Your feet, perhaps, / but, amen, Yours."

Clifton has spoken of finding the "Lucifer in Lucille," the petty part of us, the selfish part, the frightened part. Knowing those parts to exist, she reasons, "There must be a Lucille in

Lucifer." It is this stand in favor of integration that is at the heart of "brothers," that makes it the story of an individual spirit's journey in search of the union or integration with what lies beyond. There's no conclusion to the poem to speak of. The eighth and final section has the playful title ". . . . . . . is God." So there is a silence that is even beyond silence. Lucifer understands that God does speak, but in a million splintered tongues, including, he is shocked to realize, his own. He says, "to ask You to explain / is to deny You." The sin is not in questioning God, but rather in seeing God as separate, as something to be questioned at all. If God is eternal, then He must be internal, Lucille and Lucifer both suppose.

And if He isn't, if we are spirits alone in an individual universe, then there is nothing to ask, nothing that will speak back. "brothers" closes without answering any of these questions, closes in fact with a sweet moment of ultimate chaste intimacy between siblings—a kiss on the mouth—which requires silence.

NOTES

1. Lucille Clifton, *Quilting* (Brockport, NY: BOA Editions, 1991), 80.
2. Hillary Holladay, *Wild Blessings: The Poetry of Lucille Clifton* (Baton Rouge, LA: Louisiana State University Press, 2004), 138.

On the Line; or,
The Poetics of Twitter

When we talk about the line we should talk about the line separate from what came before it or after it; otherwise it is merely a sentence in prose with a break for visual effect.

Michael Palmer's "Notes for Echo Lake 4": "whose is that voice that empties."

Or Jorie Graham's "Underneath 13": "explain to me remains to be seen."

Or does the line require separate life, separate from the poem, text without context.

The line itself, ornate and gorgeous, creates a texture defined by the space between one line and the next.

What can exist in the here and now with no dependence on before or after.

Few "prose poems" seem to work with the single sentence as a carrier of poetic weight and instead work primarily with the paragraph as a basic unit, which seems to me to be just another way to frame a moment as complete but not explore the fleetingness, uncapturability and pure tragic drama of a single moment that passes and has to pass.

Hence a "prose poem" is really just prose, the beginning of an essay that a writer has chosen not to finish, or the beginning of a fiction that an American ear has not had enough guts to see as such.

Why should one bother, when working with the single line as a compositional unit in poetry, with a traditional Western structure of SUBJECT-VERB-OBJECT.

It is time for art to start re-imagining and re-orienting the conceptual understanding of the universe.

A moment needs to be seen anew.

In other words, a poem doesn't have to be a transmission from mouth to ear or page to mind but can be an encounter area.

The poetic line ought not be buckled to conventional syntax; it ought to demonstrate the actual powers of poetry to move the mind beyond the mundane, as in Jorie Graham's truncated Wyatt quote that opens "The Errancy"—"Since in a net I seek to hold the wind."

—or Broumas and Begley's ecstatic inventions in *Sappho's Gymnasium*—"Lord let me all I can wild cherry."

It ought to be able to do more, be more, transcend the pedantic definition of language as a carrier of discursive meaning and by its motion enable the mind to follow and have an understanding that is past intellectual and enters conceptual.

In my work I don't seek to move from beginning to end of a certain poem. Such predetermined motion is meant for paragraphs and stanzas.

To proceed line by line means not to feel yourself forward in the dark but to throw yourself with abandon into the arms of darkness.

Led by language, led by intuitive leaps of thought, a poem does not presume.

Not mere rhetoric or reportage or description, but pure mystery, an aspirant to the divine.

A book of poems is an abbey of aspirants, each reciting a line to herself in meditation. The lines could be heard as a chorus, in any order, simultaneously, or backwards to forwards.

Now everyone is joining in the effort of creating one-line poems, via Twitter posts.

Paul Virilio: "There is no here anymore, only now."

What he meant was a collapse of geography and distinction of place.

Or rather than collapse a conflation of all places into one place: the screen.

But what are the possibilities of a new form?

Olga Broumas: "transitive body this fresco I mouth."

Agha Shahid Ali: "of what shall I not sing and sing?"

Anne Shaw is twittering (a prettier verb than tweeting, don't you agree?—meaning is determined, after all, by sound) a project of individual one-line poems:

"help to winter me a small belief"

"i (in) visible"

"you bereft believer say you will return"

As in the court culture described in *The Tale of Genji,* poetry and letter writing each become a public art, deliciously shared and responded to.

But also allows a bravery.

One can cast a thought into the silence.

And then another.

By discrete moments, little swabs, a life can appear.

There were already twitter novels before there was Twitter. Carole Maso's *AVA,* David Markson's *Reader's Block.*

Books that use sentences and not paragraphs.

What Stein would have twittered. The thought leaves me breathless.

When I wanted to tell the story of my own life in a project called *Bright Felon,* I found I couldn't bear chapters, nor paragraphs. Sentences I could manage.

As any mode—the book, the form of the novel, the form of a memoir, blog, webpage—the modes of information distribution are created and controlled by institutions in support of state and superstate (financial) power.

But any information that flows, any communication of the individual spirit, is always counter to the centralizing urge.

So I said things in *Bright Felon* the way I could. Slowly. One thing. And then another.

If Virilio is correct and there is only a now, then wouldn't a chorus of coruscating voices from every last place in the world help us to believe once more in place, in actual human lives, bodies that really matter?

In Arabic, "word," "breath," and "spirit" are all the same: "ruh."

Yoko Ono dreamed a film in which every single person in the world smiled.

What if every human body that existed was given a chance to say a single sentence of how she felt, what he was doing, what she dreamed of.

The poet is a tricky channeler then to be able to discern music, to order the lines on a page or to seek other more transgressive models for poetry, as it occurs.

It is not that meaning is less important than music in poetry, but that when we say "meaning" we don't know what we mean.

Once more from Anne Shaw: "begin again in whether"

Ersatz Everything

The Value of Meaning

I am always in trouble because I cannot decide whether a poem is a guide toward experience that happens in the mind or inner self beyond the space of the page or human body or if a poem is inside the body or is itself the actual field of experience.

Nothing about a body is constant. Not its breath, its blood, not its skin or cells. For me nothing about a poem is constant either.

I wrote a poem called "Event," about van Gogh's painting *L'Eglise d'Auvers-sur-Oise,* a poem in pieces, twelve unrelated lines containing three narratives, a lyric musing on the pronunciation of my name and a discussion of a completely separate painting by Nicolas de Staël. There was no single "event" in the poem; I wanted instead to see the disparate lines and descriptions as a single "event" in the mind, the way Yoko Ono's *Blue Room Event* is pure script written directly onto the walls of the room in which the event does(n't) happen.

If there is an actual narrative moment in the poem, it's the story of my descent into the cold inner tombs in Saqqara, Egypt, which took place years earlier and thousands of miles distant from this place. There is something astronomical about the way the body or a poem holds experiences, all rushing away from each other at accelerating speeds.

Is that it? A chaotic world, nothing with consequence? I used to comfort myself that though all objects in the universe are racing away from each other at accelerating speeds (it's true: the speed of the universe is not—as was previously believed— constant), we were still only in the expansion half, the exhale half, one part only of God's breath that hadn't yet ended.

Meaning at some point all objects would begin rushing back to their point of origin. It was physical science and sacred scripture in happy agreement. But of course, it's not so—physicists are now re-hypothesizing that all objects may simply rush away from one other—there may be no second act, no drawing of things back together. And if we are in an eternal exhale, there must have been an initial part of creation, a part with no physical consequence at all in the universe.

Desperate to disappear, I found myself driving through the countryside from Paris to Auvers-sur-Oise, a midwinter day, cold and blue, looking for someone who wasn't going to be there, changing from a thinker to a thinker. I call myself this twice because both before and after I realized I was looking for something I couldn't find—what, Vincent alive? I knew I had too much to learn something about myself.

I want to learn something about myself because the world is real and is really ending.

Our visit to Auvers-sur-Oise felt significant. I stood at the church Vincent painted for long minutes, wondering if I should go inside. Seeing the flat sky, the monochrome landscape, and wondering, what did he see here to paint the way he did?

Because I had written the poem about the painting of the church, the painting and not the actual building became the actual object, the guide to my experience. So why shouldn't I just stand here and make pilgrimage to building alone? What does it matter whether I went in or not? Isn't the Kaaba in Mecca, direction for all Muslim prayer, actually empty inside?

"The kingdom of Heaven is within you," said Jesus, though Craig Thompson in his book *Blankets* tells that the word for "within" could also be read "among." Why not read the sentence with the doubt included, Thompson suggests: "The kingdom of Heaven is within and/or among you."[1] Are the words of a poem's experience mere receptacles for spiritual energy post-verbal, or do they enact their meanings in chemical process? What are the implications then for poetry that lives between, within and/or among various languages?

Beckett translated his own work, but not faithfully. Rather he alchemized it, transformed it. *Ill Seen Ill Said*, his self-translation of his *Mal vu mal dit*, opens, "From where she lies she sees

Venus rise. On. From where she lies when the skies are clear she sees Venus rise followed by the sun."[2] The word "on" continues to recur throughout the text as a refrain of sorts. The French word Beckett translated as "on" is "encore." The word "encore" neither connotes nor denotes "on." His translation in this case is by sound only, but not for mere play; rather, the word "on" gives an entirely new sense to the English text, a present-tense motion very different from the French text with its repetition of "encore," which can mean both "still" and "again." *Mal vu mal dit* feels thus simultaneously tied to the past and cast ahead to the unknown future, the exact opposite of living in the suspended moment of "on," a word with spatial, not temporal implications, a word which nonetheless carries (at least for Beckett or other bilingual readers) the ghost of the French word "on," an utterly untranslatable pronoun meaning at once the personal pronoun "we" and the very impersonal pronoun "one," plural in its implication, singular in its construction, both things at once.

Is art an empire of perception? When I went to the south of France, I was amazed by the way the sun brutalized objects in the landscape, how Cézanne or de Staël might have seen the physical world. De Staël chose bright turquoise for the color of the sea at least partially because at moments the sea actually *is* this color. As Cézanne perhaps painted the world in broken pieces because in the nude power of the Provençal sun it sometimes is.

Yet that day in Auvers-sur-Oise, January and gray, there seemed no hint at all of what van Gogh saw in the landscape that manifested in paintings. In other words, I suggested to myself, there *is* vision, a vision that goes beyond mere perception.

What do we have vision for now? Are we starting to sort out that global dependence on unsustainable resources like rubber and oil has gotten us into a little bit of trouble? Or that our dependence on the meat and dairy industries has something to do with global food and water shortages?

When the French franc disappeared and the euro came, we lost the bills with artists, sculptors, scientists—Monet, Cézanne, Eiffel and Marie Curie among others had graced the most common denominations of currency. I can never spend a nickel in the United States without remembering that with a single exception, all the men on our most common denominations of currency and coin were slave-owners. Two women who weren't have both been displaced for one more slave-owner.

Imagine the values of a nation, for example, whose money might depict Harriett Tubman, George Washington Carver and Emily Dickinson on the one-dollar, five-dollar and ten-dollar notes. The silver dollar coin would depict Jeanette Rankin, and the quarter would perhaps bear the likeness of Walt Whitman.

Money in this case being the metaphor for social values, perhaps not discussed but nonetheless pervasive and obvious. Beckett's text is not money for anything—since it is lost between languages, like Dickinson, like poetry, like anything sacred or secret, it can mean only itself. Cannot stand for anything, must *be* experienced.

Van Gogh spent only three months in Auvers before killing himself, so it is ironic the town has made such a killing in memory of his stay there.

His grave and Theo's, together, are an emerald ocean of ivy on which sail postcards of his paintings nestled into the leaves, messages left to him in Japanese or Korean writing, a map folded up into an origami boat. Just beyond that another grave, "Thomas LeRoy, 1980–2006, un poete." His picture is depicted on the stone; he is beautiful, smiling, kind looking.

All of this matters to me because I want to know we are actual. If the body is purely mortal and the spirit is purely immortal, do the two natures meet each other within the mind? Is there a third thing, or are three things all the self? Perhaps our obsession with these always unexpressed questions is why we pay so much attention to the body once it departs—because we know it is more than mortal, more than mere case for the "true" part of existence, that it holds its own truth, not mere church of us, but actually us also.

That we, like creation, like the universe, like a poem, like Beckett's text, can move in multiple directions at once, that space and time converge/diverge in the mind.

During my stay in France I was obsessed with graveyards. I left a copy of my novel on Duras's tomb. I felt I was publishing better than I had ever published it before. Because, having published a novel that few people read, I knew I was giving it to the one person whose approval of the book would have thrilled me, and other than that impossible approval I was tossing it into the world without attachment, merely hoping that the perfect reader—the absolutely perfect reader: someone exactly like me who would trek to the tomb of Duras on a cold Friday morning in the middle of January solely to visit—would retrieve it, would read it, would find me somehow and write to me.

It rained that night, and it is possible the book was ruined and then discarded by the cemetery workers, but a rain-soaked novel might be even more valuable to a Duras reader. Mary and I sat at the tomb of Duras, and she gave me a copy of the translation she had made of *Quinn's Passage* into French. Because we made the exchange at Duras's tomb, I remembered how I'd felt after I'd written the book: that it might be better in French, a language in which "Quinn said nothing" would not be a negation but a positive action—"Quinn se tait." Perhaps in a language in which to express negative actions you need full constructions of several words, not a single word, and in which still other concepts of negation—"nobody" or "nothing"—are not expressed in negation but as positive concepts—*personne, rien*—readers wouldn't mind a short novel of a hundred pages, a novel in which not much actually happens; character, plot and scene are all as fractured as awareness; and the writer, unable to bear finishing the plot, is permitted to not have an ending at all.

All this at the place where Duras's body was placed back into the ground. Is it a fetish for the body or for death itself that draws me always to grave sites? The actual body of Duras is down here, I kept telling myself, my palm full on the cenotaph. I could go to her house, or sit on a bench in front of a building she lived in, true, but for me the physical body is the ultimate repository, the grave the only reliquary. Hence the devastation of death and the fear that no soul-awareness remains when the body unequals itself.

All poetry is the failure to understand what happens in the body while alive, what is lost from the self at death. And it is true I do not always know what I mean, in poetry or in other languages. The best you hope for is poetry that helps you slide from one truth to another, even between languages.

Curious to read Dickinson in French. Benjamin writes that the actual inner spirit of a work—the part that is essentially untranslatable—can be fruitfully revealed in the process of translation itself, the way a new moon can be seen in the sky by looking for a circular absence of stars. Claire Malroux has accomplished a nearly unspeakable task of translating Dickinson's actual prosody into French, for example:

> Comme si tous les Cieux étaient une Cloche,
> Et l'Être, rien qu'une Oreille,
> Et le Silence, et Moi, une Race étrange
> Ici naufragée, solitaire—[3]

But Malroux understands Dickinson's sense of time and reveals it in the French better than the limitations of English allow. Dickinson uses the word "then" three times in the poem, twice as a time indicator to narrate a completed event and the third time in a more ambiguous way. The first two instances of "then"—"and then I heard them lift a box" and "and then a Plank in Reason broke"—Malroux uses the word *puis*. But for the final use of the word, the poem's ending couplet—"and hit a World at every plunge, and Finished knowing—then—"—Malroux opts for a more radical translation of the word, revealing more clearly what in English is only hinted at:

> Je heurtais un Monde, à chaque plongée,
> Et Cessai de connaître—alors—

Malroux opts for the word *alors,* implying, as I have always believed, that something else is about to happen at the end of this poem, that it ends in a fragment, ends mid-phrase. The final extremity of meaning in Dickinson's poem reveals itself most clearly in another language.

Sound can lead you, after all. First hearing it is like a river of sound, pure sound, language incomprehensible as when sitting in a train car and hearing the conversation of the people next to you, five feet, ten feet and fifty feet away, as a billowing texture matter, washing over you, drowning you, and perhaps eventually like a Hofmann painting you feel the shapes of words, phrases or at least emotional tones rising up out of the surface toward you—

Then the language is an aureole surrounding you, immediate, tantalizingly close, once discerned then perhaps poorer for the poetry of it. When one reads a book in another language, one knows well enough but not perfectly—for example, *La Palestine comme métaphore,* a collection of interviews Mahmoud Darwish gave in Arabic and Hebrew, not yet translated into English—one enters into a relationship of alienation with the text. Words like blank spaces I do not understand, grammatical constructions I have not yet learned, yet I read anyhow, reading the gaps and the words alternating like music. The sense of it, its emotional tone, its notions of alterity and alienation, I understand perfectly. Darwish lives in the space between the language he writes in and the language I write in—lives perfectly in the French I understand only at a remove.

His writings on alienation, on otherness, exile, loneliness, on the relationship between despair and political action—all come at me more truthfully and purely because they are coming through the landscape of sentences and phrases and a rhetoric foreign to me, not translated into readable English in which I can forget the miles and misery that soak the spaces between us.

So why is it that instead of art being water you swim in, with currents you might even struggle against, it's something that has to be handed to you. Beside the *eglise* of Auvers-sur-Oise, there is a big plastic placard with a reproduction of van Gogh's painting on it.

On the off chance you didn't know what you were supposed to be seeing.

At first I did not want to go inside the church at all. Isn't it a terrible thing to fill in the blank? To give yourself an answer to a mystery?

Was the church the way I had seen it—first in an image of the painting shown to me by Catherine, and then seven years later, again with Catherine, in a museum, seeing the actual painting? "Sulayman's mosque is not built of bricks and stone," Rumi said of the mythic "Far Mosque," "the farthest mosque is the one within."

So considering I'd experienced the church in my inner life, what would it mean to go inside the actual building, to see the actual world? The interior of the actual church is thrice removed from the spiritual experience I'd had seeing a postcard of the painting van Gogh made of the external walls.

Capital has used both language and spirituality to cue certain emotional responses to transition humanity from actively critical individuals to a mass entity of passive consumption. Nearly purposeless, no better than humans living in *The Matrix;* it is no fun knowing the truth—"Welcome to the desert of the real," intones Morpheus when he breaks the sorry news.

We live in a system driven first and foremost by continual growth; continual expansion and increased profit margins are structurally required. It is not "free market"—consider the roles of the Federal Reserve Bank, multinational corporations, U.S. foreign policy's primary objective during the twentieth and twenty-first centuries of preventing nations from nationalizing and controlling their own natural resources of coal, rubber, uranium, oil, nickel or canals.

So how are we supposed to sit still, even for a minute?

Visit a church, sit by the river, drink a cup of coffee, write a little note.

To be ungoverned. To know oneself actually for what one is. Actual.

Money is an exchange value system, like language. You are supposed to get what you pay for. When you say a word or use an image or sentence, particularly in public speech or advertising, you are supposed to get the equivalent in meaning. In poetry we subvert the notion of money and capital by the very nature of metaphor.

When Beckett switched "on" for "encore," he proved that when one thing doesn't equal another, new houses spring up in the neighborhood of meaning. Francs, with their portraits of painters and poets, are history, and euros, like the dollar, receive their value not from an intrinsic account but from, literally, a fiction. A dollar is a metaphor for a dollar, not an actual amount of gold metal. And even gold has no actual value; it is worth only what you are willing to pay for it; it is the antithesis of poetry, key-ing its purpose and value in precise digits to the actual price assigned by covetousness.

Capitalism is fiction that pretends to be fact. It is a fiction we all choose to believe in because we all want to eat and because we want and we want to want.

Though when I was at Auvers to look at the church, at the ordinary flat drab landscape itself, I discovered there is a reason, a reason even if it is hidden or taken for granted—as Cezanne showed the world in its shattered parts, van Gogh showed the terrifying grace of objects shattered that nonetheless (how? he never realized it at the end) hold together; each thing is not a thing, the sky hardly "sky," actually just millions of pieces of liquid or light—the actual blue in particles not waves.

But in Auvers, for van Gogh, things began to become whole again. The church quivers, almost undulates, its architecture predicting in plastic form what Gaudí would eventually actualize in stone.

In my poem "Event," I thought about this mysterious church, the confluence of events that don't seem to add up, the beauty of language and communication being its ultimate opacity. But then again, that's me: in love with silence and impossibility. My aunt Catherine educated me about van Gogh's painting of the church. The reason she loved it so much, she explained, was that the painting of the church was from the back—"There was no door, no way to get inside." You had to see it, know it was separate from you, know that there is a part of art, and by extension the human experience of the universe, that is so ineffable that you can only come into its presence, you cannot actually know it.

That's the thing Benjamin was talking about—you know it is there, a church against a sky too blue to be real, too brilliant to be looked at, but you cannot go inside.

So there I was in front of the actual church, thinking that to go inside might mar something. Because the painting of the church was more real than the actual church. The time of the painting cannot exist. The sky is a luminous brilliant blue, an hour after dusk perhaps on a clear night with a crescent moon in the sky, a blue-like sun coming through a dark stained-glass window into the interior of the church itself. The ground, the grass, is buttery yellow, high noon in the summer.

When Catherine and I stood in front of the actual painting, I reminded her of what she had said to me seven years earlier, and that I had included this observation in my poem. "No, that's not what I meant," she said. "It is true that there no doors, but look at the sky and the windows of the church." The sky was glass-blue, exactly matching the pure blue stained-glass windows. "What I meant was that because there are no doors we are always *already* inside," Catherine said. "You will have to write another poem."

Some places are impossible the way some paintings are impossible, some expressions of thought, some language constructions, actually impossible. Some constructions—for example, "Where have you gone?"—only became actual with modernity. Before that it was always rhetorical, spoken to an empty room, to someone in the presently real condition of being absent; the phrase could conceivably only be directed at a real person if you could speak to someone very far away whose location you did not know—in other words, not by letter or land-line telephone, solely by the absolutely current technology of instant-messaging or cell phone.

Encore on. These things can give time back to us. Not that we have only a moment, but that history will again unfold behind us, that the future is again possible.

That's how van Gogh's church looked. Impossible but real, a glyph for a mortal moment in the constant flux of eternity, a small word "human" against terrifying oblivion.

So standing there in the early winter light, all the colors of the landscape washed out, the sky completely unremarkably gray, I thought, better not go inside. Allow the church to be what it is, to have an intrinsic value as a sign for the always-distant-and-immediate-at-once nature of any place of worship, a phrase which in and of itself suggests a disconnect between the nature of the act and the act itself.

So perhaps with poetry as with translation and painting, you ought to do the thing with perfect awareness that the thing cannot be done. That doing can only clarify the essence of it that can't be grasped. By the attempt to transfer the untransferrable, you might limn the scope of something otherwise by definition always already absent.

Alors.

In the classics, the literature of the creation of patriarchy, often things do equal each other. You get one thing for another, and the exchange is important. Because Clytemnestra kills Agamemnon, Orestes must kill her; because he kills her, and so on. Even if the characters in the play itself do not understand or respect the value system at work, they are still governed by it. In fact, the sense of what's "tragic" is exactly that doubleness: that all things have assigned value and consequence and that the "tragic figure" is the one who does not realize or miscalculates what that value is.

Euripides pushes the envelope to extremes. Though Hecuba, for example, does seem to pay for her sin—an "act of war" not considered such because it is committed by a "civilian" and not a soldier and in "peacetime" and not during formal war (distinctions that are still quibbled over in contemporary times)— by a presaging of her metamorphosis into a dog (from a captive woman, likely headed for slavery and servitude, to a "dog of war"), it is still seen by Hecuba herself as a sort of reward—better to live as an animal than as a de-"humanized" human—or at least not as a punishment meted out for her actions but as an inevitable result of living through ten years of war, losing all of her children, including her last two after the war had supposedly been declared over. The rage of Hecuba ought to be instructive.

In *Medea* Euripides decisively cracks under the pressure of the years of endless imperial war and in exhaustion proposes that consequences are not always intrinsic to an act itself but are determined by power.

Medea, a version of a "collaborator," an Asian woman who assisted in the defeat of her people via theft of their sacred relic and murder of their prince, is betrayed herself by the imperial order. The demands upon Jason to secure the line of kingship do not include children by a colonial subject. She behaves the way powerless people in struggle must behave—with characteristic brutal efficiency. Her murder of her own children, an act that *everyone* perhaps could agree upon as "unforgivable," goes unpunished; removed from the power of men, Medea is saved by the "gods." Jason, next in line to be king, representative of mortal authority, shakes his fists impotently, shouting—in Seneca's version—the previously unutterable at the sky: "There are no gods!" even as they bear the villainess away in a golden chariot.

Medea doesn't even "sail off into the sunset" but reappears in later Greek myths, at the court of Theseus's father. She does not, in stark contrast to most figures in Greek drama, ever receive her comeuppance.

Delightfully, the actress who plays Medea also "escapes death" by sometimes returning to the scene of her crimes, not in the title role, but in the character of the Nurse. In the later performance, the audience can thus see both things happening at once—Medea speaking with her own second nature, speaking out of both sides of her mouth.

Likewise, it is the great possibility of poetry to be two or three or ten things at once. For me it's most importantly an expansion of that part of the mind that wants to limit value or understanding by time or space. On or encore.

When I was learning French, I could barely manage time. Everything was in the present tense, and since I couldn't use the subjunctive tense, peculiar clauses of possibility or tentativeness flattened themselves out into odd-sounding definitiveness. Likewise I couldn't modulate words of limitation in time or space.

Yet. Still. Unless. Until. Even though.

It is not that poetry excludes these—in fact, how could you have poetry without them—carving away from single unblinking awareness—might one say blind?—only what is right in front of one, not to the side, further ahead, or further behind, sort of like a horse; rather that in poetry there can be a kaleidoscopic awareness, a gyre of time and space where one can be all places simultaneously, as in "Saving History," collected in Fanny Howe's *Radical Love.*

In "Saving History" you are inside two awarenesses, a narrative of the story and then also an ambiguous first-person narrator who seeks to understand the story being told. Though the title of the book refers to the Christian idea of "salvation history"— that all human history is a repeating cycle of one ultimate overarching narrative of the salvation of fallen man—it also refers to the notion of saving the actual idea of history, dependant on the idea that actions have consequences after all by dispensing the old mode of history—that you have to be apart from it to tell it, or in fact, that you have to be *after* it to really tell it, an academic exercise rather of "retrieval," not "salvation."

Absolutely current technologies of computers and the Internet have enabled history to be concurrent—to be told, processed, interpreted nearly exactly as it is happening, and from the inside, by its own subjects. Winners no longer tell the tale, as evidenced by civilian blogs from Baghdad during the actual bombing or in the dispatches of Rachel Corrie from the Gaza Strip just weeks earlier.

In Howe's novel such immediate contact with the outside world is not possible: an uninsured mother agrees to traffic illegal organs across the border in order to obtain a kidney for her dying daughter. It's a particularly American story about a form of cruelty also particularly American.

We've taken for ourselves a position of empire, and like Rome mistranslating the Greek pantheon we fatally and even criminally misunderstand what is being said around us, even to our faces—tens of millions of people somehow against the most basic application of critical thought believed blank-check invasions of both Afghanistan and later Iraq to be wise and necessary courses of action. Believing also and perhaps still that it could be done without significant damage to the electrical grid and water supply and was in the best interests of the Iraqi people. All the while not understanding the most basic core beliefs of the region—believing somehow that the *wahabi* Bin Laden would support or work with the Baath Party, or failing to understand the importance of the mausoleums at Karbala.

There are no gods, cried Jason to the sky.

There is *someone*—some person—who determines value, meaning and consequence. The universe of humans does not run on its own accord. Robert Fagles talks about it in his introduction to the *Iliad*.[4] It's in Book 4 of the epic, when all parties agree to a truce—to the end of war, everything settled, the reparations agreed upon, the entire war to be personified in the bodies of Menelaus and Paris—and so agree by the way to surrender to the ruse: if Helen's body was merely the pretext for the Greeks to launch an all-out invasion of the Eastern nations, the Greeks agree now to allow the war to return to its supposed source, to relinquish their economic and political interests in controlling the Dardanelle straits in favor of the supposed actual reason for the war.

At that critical moment Athena, bent on seeing the city destroyed, pulls the string (metaphor made literal) of Teukron, a Trojan archer, kills a Greek, and with that—despite all wishes to the contrary—the war is back on.

There are no gods in the recent Hollywood treatment of the *Iliad,* called *Troy.* In it the war is driven solely by the greed of men, personified in Agamemnon. Likely it is our shifting distrust of kings in the modern age, perhaps because we understand at last that human fear is boundless and has been the source, most especially in the American century (not quite yet over), of uncountable sorrow, innumerable deaths. The godless *Troy,* with its emphasis on the roots of war being human need and greed, is a truer epic for our current age.

In Howe's novel the sinister Temple drives the story. Though Felicity surrounds herself with wise companions, including Tom, a fallen monk, and Money, a transgendered prostitute, the Magdalen to Felicity's Mary, she cannot manage to extricate herself from Temple's machinations—she struggles with this external factor governing her life.

Whether she is able to contend with it or not is the dramatic question at the heart of the novel, which frequently pauses for this type of philosophical questioning. The novel's first sentence, "Unable to rest because unable to know," lets us know that every level of how we as individuals filter and perceive our experiences will be called into question in the book.[5] Only in a novel of border crossings, of internal organs taken from one body and implanted in another, might one understand the dangerous ways we get tricked when we assume a "moral" to the story, that something is going to properly equal something else.

The cessation of active perception is a form of death, really, acceptance of passive consumption as a mode of existence.

The end of *Saving History* is a tour-de-force, utterly unexplainable; even Tom, who witnesses the events of the novel's climactic scene, is not sure what has happened. The narration dissolves. The history of it disappears—nothing happens the way you imagine it might, and in the last two pages of the book a stellar character appears and utters a single sentence, a sentence which successfully bears the weight and explains the whole of the novel which preceded it.

Writing and language can undertake the creation of cognitive space if people, like Felicity Dumas, accept as a responsibility the duty to think and critically engage not only with immediate matters but with the structures and modes of creating and marketing these "realities" to us. The solutions to problems of the state of late capital—environmental degradation and imminent permanent global wars over oil, water, food and other unsustainable resources at current rates of consumption vis-à-vis water—seem absolutely connected to the creative and critical practices of reading and writing.

Furthermore, and most importantly, a poet or novelist or writer ought to be able to have vision—to see and perceive at once, as van Gogh did at Auvers—to imagine an actuality in which the perceptual and intellectual faculties can be developed to the point of critical thinking and rejection of the extreme illogic of imperialism, separatism and war.

It is partially about being able to think in two places at once, also in two times at once. Poetry will take you to these places. Beckett attempted in the structure of prose to heighten the surface of language and lead the mind to new experiences in thought. From the experience of transcribing the polyglot *Finnegans Wake,* Beckett went one better by writing very short compressed texts. often focusing on a specific dramatic situation, the drama of which was often also in the purely emotional situation rather than the narrative, for example, in his last fictions, *Ill Seen Ill Said* and *Worstword Ho.*

Most literature, like most life experience, is filtered through memory. I am searching for art that looks forward and not merely back. This was the decisive hinge moment of which Virginia Woolf spoke, perhaps tongue-in-cheek, when she suggested human character changed "on or around December 1910." Within a few years of this date, Malevich had painted *The Black Square,* Apollinaire was writing *Calligrammes,* Stravinsky would soon premier *The Rite of Spring* and she herself had just embarked upon *Jacob's Room*, the book that would change the form of the novel forever and irrevocably. Are we likewise in a similar hinge moment?

We can finally speak in language what van Gogh did in paint—the second language of the sky, in pieces, above the *eglise*—a sky that does not exist but does is really realer than the actual sky. We don't even know "sky" until we've seen van Gogh's. To an English speaker the French *ciel* sounds solid—the ceiling of the ground really more immediate than sky, whose origins or cognates do not quite present themselves within the language itself.

You can go to a city and see only those things that already belong to you—certain monuments you have dreamed about, certain paintings you have seen pictures of or heard about—but then of course you haven't subjected yourself to strangeness at all. The actual thing itself—for example, the *eglise* at Auvers-sur-Oise—isn't real; it's only an approximation, a pale original copy of the "object itself"—that is to say, *L'Eglise de Auvers-sur-Oise*, as painted by Van Gogh. So where are you really at any moment, in a reality mediated by memory and experience? Can you actually *be* anywhere? Even in New York I long for New York, many of us mumbled in the weird months between the destruction of the World Trade Center and the beginning of the war in Iraq.

On my recent trip, feeling strange and estranged, I was asked, "Is there any place you feel most at home?" and I nearly had no answer. I was born in England and crossed the ocean in a boat. Lived first in a city, then in a trailer-park village, then in the suburbs of another country. In terms of landscape or surroundings, one place looked very much like another. Streets seemed only imitations of other streets I'd seen. Houses seemed faker than the trailers because they pretended uniqueness, but frequently one would visit a friend on another side of town and find the same house, though perhaps reversed. Minor variants of weather or native trees, all of which were planted at regular intervals in the small strip of green between sidewalk and street, were all that distinguished one from the other. I felt at home nowhere. Or perhaps more appropriately and less pessimistically, I made a home for myself wherever I went. It's either a gift or a curse, but I couldn't say which.

Food is an imitation also. Tomatoes not actual tomatoes: engineered bigger, picked raw and then sprayed with gas to tint the skin a little red. I have eaten an actual tomato in my life—the fall of 2004 at the farm on the campus of UC Santa Cruz. The farmer picked it from the vine and handed it, sunwarm, to me. I ate an actual peach once, in August 2000 in Provence, and a piece of real watermelon the following year in Egypt. It is hard to find food that is actual.

To live a life of reality, one has to work very hard. It may not be possible at all. Every object a metaphor for another. Is it possible to return to sources and original responses in the mind, attached not to preconfigured patterns of behavior but to actually being able to experience something immediate—the sunwarm tomato—for oneself?

We are so much in danger, having been taken away from our perceiving selves, converted to mere consumers of goods, good for nothing but the currency in our pockets, practically unpatriotic if we refuse to spend it. Within days of September 11, 2001, George W. Bush was on television extorting a numb American public to continue consuming.

But as much as we are committed to paying for occupation, endless war and the willful destruction of ecosystems in order to provide even more factory-farmed food, much of it to feed the global dairy and meat industries, we will neither invest in nor prize the desire to actually exist in the world, to feed and be fed by our creative powers. We accept and are willing to pay billions of dollars for the occupation, but not for adequate health care for the citizenry, superior and affordable public higher education or transportation infrastructure, all things that ought to be considered basic human rights.

Ancient people, in one of the earliest gestures of "civilization," created works of literature and performance that defined, like Adam's naming of animals, configurations of human emotion and spiritual values. Some of these ancient stories are given to us in their most broad strokes, the subtleties teased away by the eons. For example, the archetypal story of Abraham's sacrifice of his son: perhaps most important to contemporary culture is not the story itself, but rather the low-key disagreement over which son it was—in Judeo-Christian texts the named son is Isaac; in the

Quran it is Ishmael. But we spend so much time quibbling over the question of who is firstborn and thus favored we forget the actually substantive difference between the stories: Isaac does not know what his father intends in the thicket. When he arrives, bearing the wood for the sacrificial fire, he asks, "Father, where is the ram?" The climactic moment in the thicket is not the substitute of ram for son, but rather Isaac's realization of his betrayal, whether by god or his father you must decide. Ishmael, in the Islamic story, understands what will happen in the thicket; in fact, he is the one who initiates it. When Abraham, terror-stricken, recites his dream to his son, Ismail calmly says, "Do what you were commanded, father. You will find me among the steadfast."

The differences in the story offer much for contemplation and interpretation. Alicia Ostriker goes somewhat further when she suggests it is possible that Abraham failed some sort of test since the incident in the thicket marks the end of his prophethood—no further revelation is given to him. We cannot understand sacred scriptures or "secret" texts—i.e., poetry—we can only "read" them.

Surely there are signs in this for those of you who reflect. Encore. On.

But in the suburbs and the new developments, a tomato isn't a tomato, a town square is built to parody an idea of a town square, and even lakes and ponds are created to order and without geography—our pre-fab American life, panicked with nostalgia, empty of actual anything, everything ersatz.

This form of "civilization" means to take away any "strangeness"—to clear the forests, to chase away all the animals, to remove any inconvenient native people, gentrify away difference and claim the bare land for godcountry.

But even the most permanent-seeming American places are merely quivering at the seams—besides the collapse of the towers and the radical reworking of the iconic skyline so entailed, there are huge pumps in New York City working twenty-four hours a day keeping water out of the subway system and other subterranean tunnels. Paris is sinking into the ground; Venice is falling inch by inch back into the sea.

Place does not exist in time; it is actually only momentary—permanence is among the more spectacular inventions of human perception.

What we want, in poetry, in any art—because it is what we need in our lives—is to move forward into new realms of perception, new ways of seeing the sky that will prepare us for a human engagement with incredible forces of destruction, which are completely of our own design and creation. In that material sense, beyond the intangible realms of art and spirit, there are no gods.

There is no Athena plucking the bow of Teukron, but instead only flawed men without vision. We can have history back—have a past we read and understand, know the implications of both history and present action upon the future, move in both directions at once and by doing so work in support of the human spirit and against the instruments of war.

Mondrian's earliest paintings were drab landscapes, but landscapes so perfectly assembled you would cry. Blocks of color assumed physical force—the world is not imaginary but made of *things* they seemed to say. Calder too, before he abandoned the flat plane of the canvas of creation of space in air, painting modest cityscapes, the occasional pastoral, each held together so tenderly, a quivering city built of air. One admires a painter like Paul Klee, whose paintings shimmered and hovered between the abstract and the concrete, never settling on one or the other. What might have happened if Calder or Mondrian went backward as well as forward, settling neither on the mural in space nor on the tender cityscape, neither the grid of primary colors nor the drab landscape?

Malevich essentialized all representation in the supreme end of/beginning of art *The Black Square*. And then slowly, bit by painful bit, inched and clawed his way back to a form of social realism. Nicolas de Staël and Agnes Martin both likewise shivered themselves between ultimate abstraction and the incredible moment of form appearing from nothingness—the actual act of creation itself.

Was the *eglise* at Auvers-sur-Oise like that for me—a symbol of something—a place I couldn't go and so by extension a holy place, the holiest of places, a manifestation of the almost unseen? Yet, I thought to myself, I'm here in front of it, why not also go inside? Why not *actually* and finally experience it?

To go inside the church would be to simultaneously accept it as a shrine to van Gogh's vision and also to "unshrine" it, to go deeper into my own contemplation of the place itself—to make it not-fake anymore, not a metaphor for something intangible anymore, but actual.

Like van Gogh's sky, everything you look at, every word you hear, all are myriad pieces of liquid and light, too brilliantly blue to be "actual" according to rules you think you know, but there in the world, there in front of you, yes real, as real as anything.

What is it then, actual vision?

You want to wonder whether or not there are gods in the new world of a war schemed and strategized that seems now barely stoppable.

To feel that we might actually *be* in the last stages of human existence.

Are we alone among the ages of humanity in that we fear the "end of days" not because of superstition but because of hard scientific evidence?

The "end of days" isn't a metaphor anymore, but like the gem, a small figure with no real value of its own, representing only a sum of human desire, the opposite of van Gogh's church, a likewise small figure whose meaning to me is infinite.

One can name the unnameable. Jean Valentine's "Willi, Home" tells about the death of a friend. The speaker dreams of a "daffodil / lying in bed, with a sheet pulled up to its chin."[6] But far from being her ill friend, by the end of the poem, she realizes, "the daffodil / is me. Brave." In order to confront the pure horror, inevitability, finality of death, Valentine, like van Gogh, looks the thing right in the face and sees not the thing as it appears to her, not the thing as she would want to see it, but beyond human perceptions and human desires to the third thing—I believe it is real—"vision," the intersection of perception with always unattainable actuality.

Van Gogh had looked at all the objects of the world and seen their motion, the swirling energy that makes up matter, and in Auvers he painted a church that itself seemed to be melting into the ground. But the church was not melting; rather, in Auvers van Gogh began knitting the world back together.

A sky that cannot exist but which shimmers with wholeness—a sky like that, above a church with no doors, can only mean itself.

As van Gogh looked at the church and the sky and saw day and night at once, saw himself both inside and outside, the sky and the stained glass matching at once, he came into the physical presence of a unified universe—absolute and potential energy converting for a moment but eternally into each other, symbolized by us like so: ∞.

When Jean Valentine looked straight at the death of Willi, Willi dying, she loosed the lines and let the words, the very blocks of meaning, actually *mean*, without intervening syntax interrupting anything: "Brave. Willi's an iris. Brave. Brave. Tall. Home. Deep. Blue."

The blue at the end of the poem and the blue of van Gogh's sky you have never seen before. It's blue you don't know, the actualization of Stein's dream of cleaning all the junk of previous perception from words and returning them to you new, completely untouched, to be experienced for the first time in the cortex and the secret places in the brain.

What happened next? To be lost is to be found. I went inside the church.

Like many old churches, sunnier inside than you would think. White stones and wooden chairs lashed together rather than formal pews. There was a woman inside, sitting in front of the altar, playing on her guitar, singing open-mouthed but without words.

She was playing a haunting tune that I slowly realized was "Scarborough Fair." When she finished she launched into "Ave Maria." To be inside music, wordless music, I felt worldless and felt every house of god to be a house of god.

The last time I came to France, I remembered, I was constantly visiting every altar I could find, lighting candles and praying for what I thought were important things—my sisters, the well-being of the world, an end to whichever war or strife was current. And always while I was doing it, I'd feel fraudulent, as if an angel on my left hand would interrupt my prayers, plucking at my sleeve, whispering ferociously, "I know what you really want!"

What did I really want? To live in the world, to be actual, to believe it is real, that it is for something, that war and covetousness and fear are the closest things to unforgivable sins and that love is our primary responsibility as a species, the failure of which will cost us our lives, temporal and eternal both. To preserve the health and safety of the universe as I most personally know it—my own body—and to understand that body is "within and/or among" all creation in the universe.

How do you manage it—actual concern, real concern for the bodies of the world—the body of Layla al-Attar, demolished under her house by a U.S. missile launched at a military target in June 1993—"peacetime"—but gone astray to land in a residential neighborhood—the body of Rachel Corrie, four days before the beginning of the new war in Iraq, standing in front of a Palestinian home, refusing to move, buried alive in the earth?

Every stone of the city is a chapel at which I could pray, every body in the world the best sum of the meanings of all human existence, actual and eternal in only themselves.

I want, like Malevich, like Howe, like Dickinson, to be able to go forward and backward at once, like the infinity symbol; like Beckett to be able to create new experiences in language, to actually know myself; like Valentine to be actually able to see something, be actually able to speak; like Layla al-Attar, like Rachel Corrie, to know the worth and cost of the human body.

At the church of van Gogh, I lit a candle and prayed once more for the health and happiness of my sisters, and for the sake of the universe myself listened to the immensity of music without words.

NOTES

1. Craig Thompson, *Blankets*.

2. Samuel Beckett, *Ill Seen Ill Said,* trans. Samuel Beckett (London: John Calder, 1981), 7.

3. Emily Dickinson, *Car l'adieu c'est la nuit,* trans. Claire Malroux (Paris: Editions Gallimard, 2007), 99.

4. Robert Fagles, introduction to *The Iliad,* by Homer (New York: Viking Penguin, 1990), 56.

5. Fanny Howe, *Radical Love* (Beacon, NY: Nightboat Books, 2006), 313.

6. Jean Valentine, *Door in the Mountain: New and Collected Poems* (Middletown, CT: Wesleyan University Press, 2004), 167.

Write Something on My Wall

Body, Identity and Poetry

When Kara Thrace first appeared on the screen and it became clear to the audience of the new *Battlestar Galactica* that Starbuck was a woman, one first looked at the new version and thought this character was still "coded" as a "male" character—the same old wise-cracking, cigar-smoking, hard-drinking sexual predator he/she always was. Like the Cylon enemies, the body of Starbuck in the past—in this case Dirk Benedict's body—defines the body of the future Starbuck Katee Sackhoff, though she exists utterly independent of him. One's second thought was to look back at the original Starbuck character and ask whether the sexual tension between Apollo and Starbuck was always there. If you look at those old episodes, you will agree that it was. The past writes the present, for sure, but the present always returns the favor.

A body is like Dickinson's signature, which she sealed away on a separate card with her first and otherwise unsigned letter to Thomas Higginson. There are a dozen different versions of the body unfolding around the self, written and overwritten. Dickinson herself was of course overwritten—deleted and edited into limbo. She has, in a fashion, been restored, though Susan Howe's complaint that the relineation of Dickinson continues has been largely ignored—except in the Paris Press edition of Dickinson's letters to her sister-in-law Susan—and of course the bowdlerized Dickinsons of Bianchi, Todd/Higginson and Bingham are all in the public realm and continue to be widely republished; at least one edition of those is by a well-respected publisher and carries a foreword by a former U.S. poet laureate.

Of all the crew on the *Pequod* it is Starbuck who most wishes to disobey his captain. Both like and unlike his galactic counterpart, Melville's Starbuck has a strong streak of rebellion but is fundamentally part of the larger social order and continues to support it. Standing before the sleeping Ahab with a gun in his hand, for all his Christian values, he is unable to make the brutal decision that needs making—by murdering Ahab he will save both the ship and all her crew. Does the population of the ship—hence the world—die by Ahab's madness or by Starbuck's inability to act?

Higginson himself, known to us as the pompous editor, literary muck-up, distorter of genius, was actually hard at work the whole time on another issue. A dedicated abolitionist, Dickinson's correspondent put together and led into combat the first all African American regiment in the U.S. Army. Neither scholar nor mentor managed to speak themselves clearly through the shadows of history.

Is the individual body—whether Higginson's, Dickinson's, Layla Al-Attar's or Rachel Corrie's—hopeless against the tidal wave of history, the universal social action of the mind? To go back to science fiction, one is reminded of Neo from *The Matrix* trilogy. He wants to know if he has individual will at all or whether he, like those who preceded him, is condemned to make a choice based solely on his experiences and previous circumstances. In other words, is "identity" an actual spiritual concept grounded in an "individual soul," or is it, like the body, governed by a form of karma—that is to say, in the case of the soul, all of its previous experiences, which shape its emotional and spiritual and chemical responses, and, in the case of the body, all of its DNA and lineage as well as physical activities in its present life? The machinery of creation of identity seems even a bit more clear now; it doesn't need to be rehearsed or sung over and over again but rather can be cleanly assembled from do-it-yourself parts in the infinite rooms of MySpace or Facebook. And one doesn't have to engage in such creation alone; it's nearly a collaborative process, since after all: "You have 2,142 friends." In other words, the mind having always had the ability to travel at the speed of light is finally bringing the body along for the ride. Having transcended its corporeal limitations, the body flies apart in immaterial ecstasy.

This may be a particularly American or Western dysfunction. Paul Virilio writes in *The Information Bomb*, "From the beginning, the dimensions of the American state were unstable because they were more astronomical than political."[1] Ships were sent adrift across the ocean in search of any living thing, and they did not find what they thought they found. The horizon that stretched before them became, then, a national obsession—to move past sight, move past what the body could experience, to move in "manifest destiny" until it simply became impossible to move further.

Where we once thought of the mind in terms of metaphors of the body—which is to say the understanding of *corpus* was the grounding experience, the *anima* a poetic (or "astronomical") consideration—we are now moving in the other direction, that is to say, considering the body in terms of metaphors of the mind. As Virilio writes it, the *screen* has become the new version of the *horizon*, the limits of sight and perception. Unlike the horizon, however, the screen is the lip of the infinite through which anything can be seen. And of course, since "anything" can be seen, information in its infinite and supersaturated sense, it's "nothing" not "everything" that we are actually looking at.

The bodiless mind is just as dangerous in this case as the mindless body, and where does it leave us but halfway to "nowhere"?

To speak a line of poetry, a single line—to hold it in your memory, in your body and mouth, and then to sing it in the world—becomes then profoundly life-affirming, self-affirming, and so profoundly political. There is a line I carry in my head from *Sappho's Gymnasium*, by T Begley and Olga Broumas—perhaps it is even closer to my point that it is a line written by two people, a line that has passed between bodies, a communal line. The poem in its entirety, from the sequence "Vowel Imprint," runs like this: "Transitive body this fresco amen I mouth."[2]

Don't just look at it on the page; say it. Say it now, I beg you. And say it the way I've heard Broumas recite it: the consonants mere excuses, tent pegs; open your mouth on the vowels, and let your breath into the universe. The body is a functioning unit, a machine in service of energy that is neither created nor dispersed but is in eternal state of transfer. On this a poet, a Vedantic philosopher and a physicist would all be in harmonious agreement. It's not science fiction after all: matter—dark matter and antimatter included—is neither created nor destroyed.

I wonder if the purest expression of poetry is in sound and not sense. Poetry might be able to tell you something you don't even know but only if you dare not to know it. Robert Hass said it, "*blackberry, blackberry, blackberry,*" but it was in response to an intellectual drama.[3] In Michael Waters's poem, the breakup of a marriage necessitates three mantras, meant for different moments in the process, "green ash, red maple, black gum." They are like the *bhij* mantras of ancient yoga practice, in which the interior of the body can be cleaned, heightened, by the sound of the mantra itself resonating through the internal cavities.

If the purest expression of poetry is in sound and not sense, maybe the purest way of experiencing it is in a single line—a line you can chant and understand to yourself and your self. A last line like Waters's "*black gum, black gum, black gum,*" the final syllable of which is actually one of the seven *bhij* mantras, a syllable that pulls the sound and thus the energy internally and down into the root of the spine, so opposite in its aural qualities and expiation of breath than Hass's line, flooding out into the world, starting with the aspiration of the second "b" and flooding from the breath to the mouth and beyond by virtue of the liquid middle consonant "r" and the final released vowel.

What is breath after all? Not the inhale and the exhale only, but also the moments in between each. Say aloud: *Transitive body this fresco amen I mouth.*

After the initial cluster of short syllables, the line turns on the word "this"—totally empty, yet fully directive—to all the long and open spaces that follow. To me the line is out of order with regular poetic syntax. The speaking "I" comes very close to the end of the sentence. It is not fully clear what the subject, main verb and object of this line are. Is the fresco being mouthed, or the body, or is the mouth an open space at the end of the line, mere descriptor for the I? Can you diagram this line? Send all attempts to me at info@kazimali.com. I'll tattoo the most ecstatic answer somewhere on my body's blank. You'll have to study me carefully to find it.

The body is both transitive here, a passage, a bridge of flesh for breath between states of before and after, and also a fresco, made of pieces from all eras of time and all places throughout the universe. Once more, a poetic metaphor that scientists can agree upon. The word "amen" here, from Christian and Muslim prayers both, does not conclude but is rather surrounded by the present of the body and the action of the personality within it.

The line itself to me holds the best parts of poetry—music that moves through both the body and the intellect as energy, poetry that depends on the body for its expression, word arrangement that works against or outside grammar, and for an extra bonus the word "I." Rimbaud may have said "I is an other," which is very pretty, but the real problem is that I really *isn't* an other, is it?

Dickinson's textual body was literally broken to pieces by the hands of two women, her brother's wife and her brother's lover. The daughters of these women continued the practice. No matter what kind of work R. W. Franklin did in matching ragged paper edges and watermarks to one another, some secrets keep themselves. More interesting perhaps is Marta Werner's textual work with the scraps and fragments that remain. What Werner does is read the surfaces—the actual body as it exists today.

In fragment A638a in Werner's cataloguing, on a small bit of paper, Dickinson writes a shocking manifesto to the future of the body of poetry:

> We do not think
> enough of   the
> Dead as   Exhili
> rants   they are
> not   dissuaders
> but   Lures—
> Keepers   of   that
> great Romance
> still to us   fore
> closed— while
> we   Envy   their
> wisdom   [   ]
>   lament

> Coveting their wis
> dom   we   lament
> their   Silence
> Grace is still
> a secret—[4]

The untranscribed word following the first "wisdom," to my eye, is either "made" or "nude," interesting in either case. Still the spacing, the lack of hyphens in the cut words, the stumble and stutter and re-start are things I love the most about both this Dickinson text and the practical existence of the individual human body.

But it gets better than this, better than I can adequately reproduce here, because written vertically in the gaps between words in the text are two additional couplets. The first, running down the left portion of the page, reads: "That they still exist / is a / trust so / daring." It cuts the Dickinson text in two vertical columns to create a subsection along the left margin that reads: "We do / enough / Dead / rants / not / but / Keepers / great / still / closed / we / wisdom // Coveting / dom / their Grace / a." Even cut to pieces, when it is by her own hand and her text left otherwise unedited, Dickinson is brilliant. Along the extreme right margin of the paper is another couplet that reads, "that they have existed—none / can take away." Indeed, the human body holds deep its own suppressed experiences, its own revisions, even the cells of its very flesh, even when the sophisticated mind plays every trick in order to forget.

In the secret and confused texts of Dickinson's fragments, one can be lost in the language, be dizzied in it, seduced by it, distressed or dreamed of. To quote Broumas and Begley's "Vowel Imprint" one more time, "Where I unbind my hair light's first blue witness." As in Dickinson, I begin to suspect it is the lack of punctuation and its determination to lock down the syntax of a phrase that allows the language in these scraps to sing.

I suppose what makes Broumas and Begley's work in *Sappho's Gymnasium* so compelling is that the fragments are intentional, and they are oral. As such they bridge the gap between the irretrievable lost history of the woman writer and the embodied present in which the scraps and fragments that remain still live and blazingly so. Fragments spoken like this carry the height of meaning, a space between the reader and writer that is so dizzyingly intense that one—whether reader or writer—has no choice but to stutter or moan.

What was it Icarus saw on his way plummeting down to the ocean's surface? Or Pip the cabin boy, in *Moby-Dick,* hanging on to the tarred-up barrel for a day and a night, a castaway, inch by inch going silently mad? What made Pip mad was his vision of the absolute horizon through the day and the night—he came to perceive the dizzying infinite, God's foot on the treadle of the loom of creation, but what he saw was the vastness of nothingness.

The horizon of nothing is what we, in American obsession, came to the edge of eventually. In fact, once this occurred, once we had fulfilled our "manifest destiny," it seemed, as Virilio wrote, that "the history of the United States seemed to be completed, seemed halted at the outer limit of the continent, on the horizon of the Pacific."[5] Did it seem inevitable then that we would eventually push further, occupying territories in the Pacific and Alaska? The occupation of the Philippines at the beginning of the twentieth century marked the beginning of this imperialist project, one that continues today. America, as Virilio continues, was "still hungry—not so much for territories as for trajectories; hungry to deploy its compulsive desire for movement, hungry to carry on moving so as to carry on being American." One could infer also that this American restlessness within the polity is mirrored by restlessness in the individual body. As Jean Baudrillard writes in his book *America:* "All these track-suits and jogging suits, these loose-fitting shorts and baggy cotton shirts, these 'easy clothes' are actually old bits of nightwear, and all these relaxed walkers and runners have not yet left the night behind. As a result of wearing these billowing clothes, their bodies have come to float in their clothes and they themselves float in their own bodies."[6]

What's happened is the end of locality, the end of the body, the end of actual physical existence in the world and the beginning of pure concept—how can we even be where we are? One extreme is the human bodies in *The Matrix,* not at all where they are, but stacked like eggs at the supermarket, plugged in like the batteries for consumption that they are. How different is this from the cyberreality of Facebook? At the other extreme you have the lost exile adrift in a world without place; as Edmond Jabès explains it, you are never really anywhere, because everywhere you go you have brought all the places you have left with you.[7] In an increasingly electronic world, where information is in constant feedback with events themselves unfolding, Virilio even argues: "Here no longer exists. Everything is now."[8]

When Pip looked out at the horizon, he saw nothing and went mad. The American empire itself continues to thrust its hands out, reaching, reaching to infinity. But the globe, cyberspace notwithstanding, is not infinite. At some point, arms reaching out will meet one another. No one on the ship bemoans the loss of Pip, remember. He is found by accident, and once he displays his eerie poetic rants, no one wants anything more to do with him. It is Ahab ultimately who takes the gibbering child under his wing and, in a fashion, rehabilitates Pip by ushering him into an embrace of his madness.

Of course Pip did not see the nothingness of the horizon. In fact the horizon led him to the new horizon in his own delirium, Virilio's "screen." Pip imagined himself sinking below the surface of the ocean into the unknown depths, where he saw not nothingness but the wondrous shapes of infinity. It was the infinite of the screen, not the absolute absence of the horizon, that revealed to him the figure of God and ultimately drove him out of his mind. "Man's insanity is heaven's sense," Ishmael remarks.

To go inside one's mind, through visions and sound, is a great gift. No one does it like Andrew Joron. His vowels fold and unfold into and out of one another, all along maintaining the greatest intellectual engagement. His poem "Materialism," from his new collection *The Sound Mirror,* opens:

> Failed fold
> > makes the cut continuous—
> Unclosed is
> Unclothed
> > in the drama that Thou art
>
> > outward the word (outside
> > —interstellar costume—
> > > the fits of a dress).[9]

What he enables the poetic line to do is to have a thousand lives, combining and recombining in sound, sometimes being echoed several lines later. It's Steinian in its treatment of language as plastic material, Dickinsonian in its creepy inquiry into the nature of the relationship between individual identity and the outer world, and Barbara Guest—like in its sheer playfulness and joy in poetry (who would have expected that "interstellar costume" to show up?).

Though the sound pattern does nothing *but* repeat, Joron continues:

> Unrepeating pattern
>
> Where
> X relaxes relation, where
>
> X licks the elixir of
> night's rhyme with light.

"X" here perhaps means the unknowable in the equation of identity—where does it come from, how is it constructed? In the first mathematical guess, the unknowable of "identity" might release the stress of knowing the difference, but in the second, the "X" knows the answer is found in pure ecstatic engagement with the senses.

It's the senses we've stopped depending on. As our information-gathering facilities slowly transform from biological and internal to technological and external (and threaten now to transform again to technological and internal!), it is our corporeal form itself, the human body, that Virilio argues is the last frontier, "which has at all costs to be invaded or captured through the industrialization of living matter." Small wonder, then, that while the science fiction of the forties, fifties and sixties was obsessed with the political Cold War, that of the seventies and eighties and early nineties with disasters on a global scale (Žižek argues in *Welcome to the Desert of the Real* that a society in such extreme excess as ours actually *dreams* of the disaster, is secretly just waiting for it to happen), science fiction of the late nineties and new millennium is obsessed with the individual human body, how it can be colonized, changed, subsumed.[10] Whether a Terminator, a Cylon or a hapless human caught in the Matrix, we are not who we say we are, are unable to assert our own human essence in the face of technological expansion.

In fact, this human panic is built into all of the science fiction dealing with the trauma of the clash between technology and civilization. The Cylons, constructed by humans, believe in their own souls as created beings. In this they are a re-boot not of the original *Galactica* series, but actually of Victor Frankenstein's creation, now so caught up in the destiny of his creator, he has taken on even his name. The villainy of Victor Frankenstein in Shelley's novel is not in his creation of life itself, but in his refusal to take responsibility for his creation and teach him. While his initial refusal results in the textually ambiguous—in terms of intention—death of William Frankenstein, it's the later refusal to provide the creature with his companion that turns the creature truly murderous.

What Victor never manages to do is confront his own creature and accept responsibility for his own actions. At the heart of the technological disaster is always the spark of human that made it so, because in poetry you can always speak in riddles, say one thing and then another, the chains of logic in poetry like the dual paths in the body, motion of inhale and exhale, talking out of both sides of one's mouth and offering a new way of understanding the flickering and mortal world.

To assert humanity and the validity of the human experience seems terribly important; otherwise the bodies of humans disappear into the drift of history and political events, the way Rachel Corrie's body disappeared, or Layla Al-Attar's—flesh and bone, destroyed physically, certainly, but also banished and vanished in the sea of information in constant production. Dickinson wrote her name on a small card and sealed it up in a tiny envelope, including this with her otherwise unsigned letter sent to Higginson.

How small one can make oneself inside one's own mind. In the section "Parables," from his sequence of poems "Two Suitcases of Children's Drawings from Terezin, 1942–44," Edward Hirsch makes several turns using sound and the line break to heighten the emotional intensity, as if he were delicately opening signatures sealed in an envelope. These were real children, kept in a concentration camp designed to prove to visiting officials that the Nazis were not persecuting Jews. The very unreality of the concept (the children were eventually all killed) represents the same disconnect between war and the individual body, death as represented in news reports and empty numbers and actual bodies on the ground. Hirsch writes in one section, "All night the girl / looked out the window / until the window disappeared / and there was no girl."[11]

Just as there is a confusion between what is real and what is imaginary, the children cannot remember their previous lives or experiences: "No one in dormitory L410 remembered / if the Talmud was written / in black letters on white fire / or in white letters on black fire." The truth implicated in the confusion is more sinister than the merely poetic; in such an atmosphere a prison camp, whether a "model camp" or no, has real import: "She painted herself light blue / when she felt like a flute // She painted herself dark blue / when she felt like a cello // She painted herself black and blue / when she was bruised into silence."

Here in a camp where young Jewish children were given music lessons, dance lessons, art lessons, then ushered quickly to their deaths, even the imaginary holds real menace: "He drew a German shepherd inside a cage / and blacked the cage with a crayon // It was sealed shut / but he could hear the dog barking at night."

Hirsch creates the sense of severe disconnect between what one can say and what one can understand in two remarkable couplets near the end of the section. In the first, a simple word shift, as in Andrew Joron's poem, opens up a new road to understanding: "We did not make graven images / we made images from the grave." In the second he uses a line break in a repeated phrase to contradict the earlier message of hope:

> Someone wrote in tiny letters in pencil
>
> *I don't believe God forgot us*
>
> but someone else scrawled in thick letters in pen
>
> *I don't believe*
>
> *God forgot us*[12]

This one line in dialogue with itself takes on haunting and awful meaning here as manipulated by Hirsch, and to me this is the richness of the body—breath that moves into and out of itself, and words that move among one another, turn each other over to create new rooms of meaning. In this I am very attracted to the non-linearity and intertextuality of the Internet the way it is currently constructed. Icons open and lead into one another, and after five minutes of wandering you are a million miles from where you started. Virilio's screen is frightening, yes, but dizzy with possibilities as well. Though Baudrillard warns that when *everything* means *something*, then nothing means anything.

Is it true? Are we drenched in signification? I saw a reality show once about who was going to be interesting enough to get a reality show of their own. In sheer terms of semantic madness, my favorite reality show title is *Paris Hilton's My New BFF*. The final "F" is supposed to stand for "forever" which obviously doesn't mean what it used to mean if the adjective assigned to it is "new." Upon dismissing the contestant of her choice at the end of each episode, Paris bids them farewell by saying, "TTYN," a cruel though funny emendation of the online sign-off "TTYS." It's not smart just because it is bringing cyberreality into the actual world (which in the first place is a metaphor—no one actually "talks" online), but also because it contains the paradoxical act of "talking" but "never."

Small wonder, then, that I trust Paris Hilton and Jean Baudrillard both—precisely because we have entered an age of true gaps and spaces between words and what they mean, the possibilities of poetry have increased a thousand-fold. It's a dream to me to be lost in the space between a noun and the verb that goes with it, especially if those two are separated by several words or even a poetic line.

In early 2007, I was at the railing of the cliff beach at Santa Cruz, California. I had just learned the night before of the passing of Alice Coltrane. Shocked and feeling very lonely, I was watching the waves hit the red rocks and disappear instantly into tons of mist. Racing on the surface toward the rocks—who knows how they rescued themselves before striking them—were surfers, balancing on their boards, crazy in the wind. I loved the image of a human being—a soul inhabiting a body—as a surfer traveling on the very edge of the infinite; the joy of their experience was traveling atop it, not immersing themselves in it. One surfs the Internet as well, and one feels this most modern of textual conglomerates has much more in common with the ancient forms of literature than we imagine.

Jonathan Rosen writes of the connection between, of all things, the Talmud and the Internet: "Vastness and an uncategorizable nature are in part what define them both . . . Nothing is whole in itself but where icons and text boxes are doorways through which visitors pass into an infinity of cross-referenced texts and conversations."[13] Rosen goes on to describe the various conversations and arguments that emerge and re-emerge, cross-reference and continue a conversation "that began two thousand years ago" and "is still going on in pretty much unbroken form."

We haven't yet begun to explore what it means for our language and our sign-making processes to now have access to such meaning-making mechanisms as website home pages, blogs, Facebook walls, YouTube and who knows what other democratic avenues will open themselves into the future. But considering class issues surrounding access to these technologies, and the political and corporate hands that move behind the distribution of information, one wonders if we will continue to homogenize our language and culture in an as yet unheard of manner, travel closer and closer to being humans plugged into the Matrix, or mere minds without corporeality simply "downloaded" into our bodies, or will we somehow manage to fracture into fabulous new Babel?

It is not new, this intertextuality, the moving of understanding from one locale to another, but perhaps what is new—and sinister—is the degree to which economic power determines access to new information media. The other problem that presents itself is the problem of "knowing." While poets—the ones I love anyhow—have always eschewed certainty, the wide prevalence of mass media has only hardened the notion of fixed meanings, not dissolved it. Witness the ease with which the United States was ushered into global war. Our exit from it and a move back toward peace-making depend solely on our releasing the notion that "we know best," surrendering—at last!—the doctrine of American exceptionalism.

Dickinson herself finished with "knowing" in her poem "I felt a Funeral in my Brain" but left that enticing "then" as the single word on the final manuscript line. Dickinson, typically cagey, doesn't say what happens *after* "knowing" is finished. At least not right away. Dickinson, that gardener of plants and poems, takes a cutting from this poem and attempts to grow another poem from a variant line reading "I felt a Cleaving in my Mind." It's not the only time, of course, she's subbed in nouns and verbs but left the syntactic structure intact.

Each concerns itself with "knowing"—the first is the narrative of how one dispenses with the requirement to know, the second a lyric that tells what the experience *feels* like. In another sense "I felt a Cleaving in my Mind" is also a meditation on the ability of lyric to revisit its subjects. Dickinson sent the second stanza of this poem in a letter to Susan, though the first couplet in this version does not read, "The thought behind I strove to join / unto the thought before," but rather, "the Dust behind I strove to join / unto the Disk before."[14]

Of course Dickinson was not the only one who subbed words for words in her poems. In the final couplet of the second stanza she writes:

> But Sequence ravelled out of Sound
> Like Balls—upon a Floor.

To me, the word "sound" is key here—meaning progresses from it, the word "ravelling," like the word "cleaving," meaning both a thing and its opposite. It's this single word also that Dickinson's editors subbed out for the 1896 edition of her poems, rendering the line instead, "But sequence ravelled out of reach / like balls upon a floor." Something that "ravels out of sound" might at first appear to be a fair definition of the poetry of Joron or Broumas and Begley. Sound, for Dickinson, has echoes of both sources of poetry and unknowability. In a poem she wrote in between this pair of poems, Dickinson again considers the actual materiality of the mind, first as a metaphor but eventually actualized in a physical form, the chosen form again being "Sound":

The Brain—is wider than the Sky—
For—put them side by side—
The one the other will contain
With ease—and You—beside—

The Brain is deeper than the sea—
For—hold them—Blue to Blue—
The one the other will absorb—
As Sponges—Buckets—do—

The Brain is just the weight of God—
For—Heft them—Pound for Pound—
And they will differ—if they do—
As Syllable from Sound—[15]

In this poem Dickinson compares the brain to both the sky and the sea; in each case the brain is reckoned superior, not for its mass but for its ability to "contain." "The Brain is just the weight of God," Dickinson says, the two hefted physically and found to differ, "if they do," only as much as "Syllable from Sound." "Syllable" is the container by which humans expel the larger and more abstract "Sound." Led by language, Dickinson does not allow the "funeral" in the brain to be the end, but rather only the beginning of an unreeling sequence of poetic thoughts that comment back, embellish and sometimes contradict what came before.

The human body, as Virilio wrote, is the last frontier, and it's the experiences of this body, like Pip's adrift on the surface of the infinite ocean, that can lead us to greater understanding. Joron concludes his poem "Materialism" with these lines:

Possessor, picture
Bare chamber—
      stain instead of identity

      the plait of, the plaint of

      simple.

Thou thousand, imitation
Shadow[16]

The argument he makes here about identity—being traces left behind, a "stain"—plays itself out in the arena of sound.

The individual is not only multiple but also barely there, barely real.

So is that it? Does the "transitive body" have any chance of actually existing in the world, understanding itself? For Neo and the others caught in the Matrix it is the simple matter of a pill. Our actual world is perhaps more complicated. There is a rapture in the movement of the mind and the body that can only be duplicated in language, not in spite of the stark gaps that have opened between word and meaning, but perhaps *because* of them. Subject to colonization, subjugation, invasion on every level, each body has only what it is made of.

The beautiful wisdom of Broumas and Begley's line coruscates in and out of me as if it were breath: *Transitive body this fresco amen I mouth.* The body here is a "fresco"—the eternal matter painted into the flesh and surface of the body. You can see creation as an alert flickering on your screen: "Someone has written on your wall." But the line includes two further motions, one of the individual internal—"amen"—and one of the individual actualizing herself into the external world—"I mouth."

As Dickinson found sequence ravelling out of sound, as Pip noticed in the infinity of space and in the timeless passage of a day and a night adrift, we may find our best spiritual, intellectual and emotional nourishment not in the expected, in the plain-spoken or in the linear, but in the conflicted, confused and vexed spaces of the oral and ecstatic, the profound and the difficult.

NOTES

1. Paul Virilio, *The Information Bomb,* trans. Chris Turner (London: Verso, 2005), 21.

2. Olga Broumas and T Begley, *Sappho's Gymnasium* (Port Townsend, WA: Copper Canyon Press, 1994), 77.

3. Robert Hass, *Praise* (New York: Ecco Press, 1979), 5.

4. Emily Dickinson, *Open Folios,* ed. Marta Werner (Ann Arbor: University of Michigan Press, 1995), 95.

5. Virilio, *Information Bomb,* 22.

6. Jean Baudrillard, *America,* trans. Chris Turner (London: Verso, 1989), 39.

7. Edmond Jabes, *A Foreigner Carrying in the Crook of His Arm a Tiny Book*, trans. Rosmarie Waldrop (Hanover, NH: Wesleyan University Press, 1993), 125.

8. Virilio, *Information Bomb*, 125.

9. Andrew Joron, *The Sound Mirror* (Chicago: Flood Editions, 2008), 7.

10. Slavoj Žižek, *Welcome to the Desert of the Real* (London: Verso, 2002), 17.

11. Edward Hirsch, *Lay Back the Darkness* (New York: Alfred A. Knopf, 2006), 51.

12. Ibid., 54.

13. Jonathan Rosen, *The Talmud and the Internet* (New York: Farrar, Straus and Giroux, 2000), 7.

14. Emily Dickinson, "I felt a Cleaving in my Mind," in *The Poems of Emily Dickinson*, ed. R. W. Franklin (Cambridge: Harvard University Press, 1998), 812.

15. Emily Dickinson, "The Brain is Wider than the Sky," in *Poems*, 595.

16. Joron, *Sound Mirror,* 8.

Why We Need Poetry Now

Poetry, to me, is an art that lives in the body—in its cavities of breath and mechanisms of propelling breath, in the vibrating cords of voice, deep in the skin and blood, and flashing across the axons and dendrites deep in the brain's neural networks. If it seems political in the extreme, it is because throughout what we call human civilization, but at no time more intensely than at the present moment, the individual body has been under attack by collective bodies—the body politic, the corporation, various strains of organized religion that all at least agree on one thing: salvation requires the individual to submit his body to the law.

The ability of humans to organize themselves into communities along common identities beyond the national or religious, common ways of thinking, artistic, linguistic or cultural practices, has always been threatened by a hegemonic and centrist element. Witness the recent puzzling backlash against gay marriage in "the land of the free," which is itself intent on bringing "freedom" to all the dark spaces of the world.

I think about two bodies over and over again, in waking life and in my dreams—the bodies of Layla Al-Attar and Rachel Corrie, women murdered by state violence ten years apart but in the same part of the world.

One of these women was middle-aged, married and a mother; the other was young and idealistic, at the beginning of her life. One woman was an Arab, an internationally known artist, who spent her life creating paintings, curating exhibits and traveling the world to promote art and artistic expression; the other was a college student, fighting and advocating on behalf of the most powerless members of the community she was living in at the time of her death. One of these women put herself—quite literally—in the path of danger; the other slept in the night, with no idea what was burning in the skies above her. One felt the lip of the metal bulldozer against her body; the other drifted in consciousness when the nose of the missile first entered the roof of her house.

Layla Al-Attar's body evaporated, combusting in fire, consumed; Rachel Corrie's body was first broken and then folded down into the soft earth of the construction site.

The war—as an abstract concept, not a local political situation—is still on, though the new administration has changed the vocabulary, and the terror threat level has been lowered to yellow; it will always be on, I'm afraid, so long as the flow of capital is permitted to be more important than the flow of breath in the individual respiratory systems, blood in the individual circulatory systems, food and water through the digestive systems of all the billions of individual bodies on the planet.

Poetry is the smallest way—it is a small, small way, but it is a way indeed—that the individual body can express its own personhood and value in the face of faceless systems. They are called faceless because in becoming collective they believe they are "embodying"—i.e., becoming a "corporation" or a "body politic"—but really they are disembodying, disemboweling themselves, dehumanizing themselves. Thus having become inhuman, they have no other choice but to subvert anything human to the bottom line of dollar, God or pure power.

I do not know if I will ever be as brave as Rachel Corrie, shouting in the very face—literally—of the driver of the bulldozer which knocked her down. Layla Al-Attar's death, on the other hand, was karmic coincidence; she could no more avoid it than Rachel could avoid her own, though Layla was killed by surprise, in the dark hours of early morning, her house destroyed, her paintings in flames.

In poetry, in community action in solidarity with the disempowered, unhomed, dehumanized, in the trust of a human expression in a human mouth, we might start moving toward a consciousness beyond the individual that is grounded in selfless action and not selfishness, greed and acquisition.

The water on the planet is being used at an unsustainable

rate. Much of the fresh drinkable water is being used to feed animals raised solely for consumption; much more of it used for the production of silicone chips necessary for production of electronics. The global food distribution system and its dependence on dwindling fossil fuels is in danger of imminent collapse.

We need new solutions.

Of what use is poetry in a time of multiple collapses? We need to construct a new value system, one that prizes the individual and human, that eschews needless desire and has a view of interconnectedness of all living things, based not on the flow of money, but on mutual interest and, yes, kindness.

Faith and Silence

I remember the churches in the Coptic quarter of Cairo—underneath the ground, a dark staircase to the side of an empty courtyard, nearly overlooked. The entire church existed in the dark under the streets of the quarter. In that ancient city of a thousand mosques, some faith stayed silent about itself.

In Luqman:27, the Quran tells us, "even if all the trees in the world were made into pens and all the oceans in it made into ink, with seven more oceans to multiply it, still the words of God would not come to end." It's what poets dream about—that the entire universe is never-ending revelation and everyone with their ear to the ground—literally—might luck into prophecy. Still, with all the countless men and women in the beginningless generations who have "heard" the words of God in the rain, the wind, the stones, or from angels, we haven't managed to still the storm in the world or in our hearts.

"The Quran mentions one hundred and four revelations but only four of them by name," my wise father told me once. The four? The Torah, the Quran, the Injeel—a text revealed to Jesus, but now believed by Muslims to be lost—and the Zubuur (psalms) of Dawud. And the other hundred books? "We don't know their names," my Dad says. "So the Baghavad-Gita could be one?" I ask him. "It could be," he agrees. In this way he taught me respect for all traditions of the world, but also respect for mystery itself—the one hundred missing books equal the one hundred names of god. And "one hundred" itself perhaps only a metaphor for all the trees and oceans of the world?

For me, how you talk to God is paramount. I first learned to pray in another language I didn't understand. I was taught syllables first by transliteration and then in the Arabic original. It was hard work getting my tongue wrapped around the Arabic vowels and consonants that do not exist in English. Like the consonant in the middle of my first name and the vowel at the beginning of my last name, expressions of faith were unpronounceable.

My favorite of the five daily prayers was the first because you prayed it early in the morning before dawn, usually before anyone was up, in the privacy of your own room. As far as prayers go, though you were reciting out loud, they were secret. My next favorites were the noon and afternoon prayers because for some reason these prayers are supposed to be recited silently. Your lips move so people know you are in prayer but you make no sound.

For so many generations faith needed to be secret, under pain of torture or conversion. Silence is different than secrecy of course, but like the one hundred and four books, we cannot know the truth of our faith. And if we can then there's no "faith" to it; such faith has all the charm of reading a dictionary.

Because I couldn't speak to God properly—I learned to speak to Him by rote—I drifted away from prayer as an idea of speaking to God ritually and toward different forms of worship: meditation, yoga practice, and a perhaps odd habit of talking to God or an empty room the way you might talk to your friend at the coffee shop.

A drone in music often accompanies yogic chanting or meditation. It's a single note held and maintained. Often times if you listen carefully to it you can hear the harmonic sounds under the note—you can hear infinity in the singularity, as in David Lang's *The Passing Measures* or Sheila Chandra's *ABoneCroneDrone* series. The sound is supposed to organize or focus the practitioner on the inner sound—called "nada" in Sanskrit. I always liked that this same word means "nothing" in Spanish because nada is nada—no thing at all in the heart of awareness.

Not to say that there *aren't* "things" but after all, then again, maybe there aren't.

For some time I have been in love with the paintings of Agnes Martin. Not with the blankness of them at all, but with the human touch, with the coolness, the emptiness of mind that can approach a canvas and lightly touch it. Each small gesture, each motion on the surface seemed so silent and thus an incredible vessel of human emotion and communication. I find her canvases deafening in their concurrent embrace and refusal of simplicity, their motion, their restraint. You only think there's nothing there, but there's something there, something solid and real. Cage taught us that there is no silence—especially not these days of intense electromagnetic radiation blanketing the air—and there never was.

Besides, it seems like any time someone thinks they have heard God whispering to them through the silence, there's trouble in it for someone.

I think it's why I began to be attracted to poetry that was quiet about what it believed. Jane Cooper's work, for example, is haunted by the fleeting nature of a human life against the immortal scale of not God or a Creator but rather *Creation*, as if for Cooper the maker is in the made. "To live to be a hundred / is nothing," she writes in "Winter Road," "the landscape is not human / I was meant to take nothing away."[1] Her poetry always acknowledges that there is something that cannot be said, questions about existence that will not or cannot be answered. Earlier she writes, "birch leaves // make a ground bass of silence / that never quite dies."[2]

Talking to God is always essentially talking to Someone Who isn't going to answer. And for many of us it is talking to Him in languages we do not understand. Most people pray looking at their own hands. The body perhaps being the soul's ultimate fetish object. The body is the mortal part, the case of existence that the soul can look to for proof it is "real," that the world is actual. And of course—the urge is at the root of religion—the body looks at the soul in wonder, desperate for proof that there is more than the world, that there is some form of immortality, that death of the body is not annihilation of the soul or self, whatever those two things are.

In the Siva Samhita, an ancient Yogic text, it is written, "As in innumerable cups of water, many reflections of the sun are seen, but the substance is the same; similarly individuals, like cups, are innumerable, but the vivifying spirit, like the sun, is one" (Siva Samhita I:35). It's as if in human life as in poetry there is an electric current in the air that animates each individual body or poem that is entirely unique and beyond the fleshly or verbal confines of that individual construct.

Or as Donald Revell expressed, you don't find poetry in poems.[3] Because every poem—every effort at putting the ineffable into language—is destined to fail.

If there are a hundred unmentioned books in the world, it stands to reason, my father thought, that all peoples of the world, in all various times, must have had revelatory texts—why would anyone be left out of salvation, he wondered? It's an ecumenical Islam that I adore in him. "All rivers go into the same ocean," my grandfather was fond of saying on the question of religious tolerance. I thought him incredibly wise to have thought of such an image; of course I later found that particular quote in both the poetry of the sufi poet Hafez and the philosophical writings of Swami Vivekananda. Vivekananda may have read it in Hafez, and I hope my Muslim grandfather found it there in his Vedanta writings.

But it's a one-way conversation, the idea of prayer. You talk to God. God is silent. You read the silence. For some people the holy texts are God talking back. Some people know the texts so well they can quote any part they find relevant to any daily situation. There are divination methods using the text to discover answers to daily dilemmas. Does it strike you as odd, a way of putting words into God's mouth? So much depends on the belief then of absolute purity of transmission of those texts. The titular metaphor of Rushdie's novel *The Satanic Verses* was an imagined situation of a corrupted holy text. Mayhem ensued in art as in life.

The trauma of a prayer is not merely that we are forced into such a desperate situation as having to beg for something, but in the ultimate lack of an answer. Should the prayer be fulfilled we take it as an answer and if the prayer is not fulfilled we try for the justification: that God had other plans. But how might a god "answer" the prayer of a parent of one sick child but not another? You would say, "It was in God's plan," in which case we have to admit no one "answered" any prayer, but that events unfold beyond their pale.

In any case the rhetoric of prayer leaves the supplicant in a poor position indeed—we are powerless creatures, on the outside of Divinity, with no concrete influence on it whatsoever. No wonder children and adult alike prefer stories of youngsters—with broomsticks and spidersuits, wardrobes with doors to other worlds, or horcruxes that can hold the mortal spirit—to the watery vestments of faith, whatever it is.

Only some poems talk about life, describe objects and experiences. Other poems dream of music, dance, and prayer—like the wisteria in Lisel Mueller's "Monet Refuses the Operation," sometimes you find a poem that "becomes the bridge it touches."[4] It's a brave supplicant that continues to speak in the face of silence.

Revell goes on to suggest that one does not find "poetry" in poems, but that a poem is what is left after "poetry" has passed through a place. There is some ineffable experience that we might try to write about or describe, but often the experience itself remains slightly beyond the ken, the way one must not look directly at the sun, the way one must not, in some traditions, speak the name of God. We are left with its trace, a footprint, a curtain swaying with the breeze of someone's passage.

But how could I be a poet, how could I pray at all, when there was something I wasn't telling anyone, even God? Isn't absolute silence the thing that won't answer, the one thing you can trust, that you can tell anything to? But I couldn't even do that much. Ultimately it was my unwillingness to speak about the one thing perhaps most important in the mortal and carnate universe—my body's desire—that torqued my language into poetry. I never knew how to say anything directly and so I had to hedge in a hundred different ways.

It's naïve to say this hedging in poetry did not carve a landscape in my ability to express anything or even my ability to think through things in my actual life.

To me Islam was never about the absolutes or the adherence to one interpretation of it—indeed it splintered almost immediately upon delivery. The one verse that was repeated over and over again in the Quran that I loved the most was "Surely there are signs in this for those of you who would reflect." The fact that this verse is used rhetorically and poetically causes many to miss its actual practical application: active engagement in matters of faith.

But I'm not to be trusted. I can talk about faith and silence in poetry and metaphor a million times but the most intimate of my self's secrets—love and desire—remained utterly separated for so many years from the most intimate of my body's partners in the world—from the seed and soil it came from, from the places it was brothered to.

When I learned to talk to God or to Silence, the lack of response was key to my willingness to speak at all. If God was never going to respond to me I would have to figure out Heaven for myself—I would have to know not by book but by heart what I believed and where I was bound. The Quran with its constant repetition of mysterious stories with various small and large differences, followed by that ubiquitous repeated verse—"surely there are signs in this for those of you that reflect"—seemed to back me up.

When you sit in a darkened room, talking to no one even headlights on the street a hundred feet away seem to be happening right next to you.

Some years ago I lost a manuscript of poetry. Forty original pages, handwritten, not copied, not typed up, not anything. What I could reconstruct I reconstructed from earlier drafts, from memory, from prayer, and sometimes from dream. When I lost my folder of poems, I received so many different forms of advice. Robin said that the loss itself would change my writing practice. Gray said that I should write to the silent place itself. Marco said even if I couldn't remember the poems' words, the experience of writing them had already changed me, was already in my body. So it would be possible to rewrite those poems just from memory. Even if the "poem," the trace-record of poetry as Revell says, was gone or utterly different, the "poetry" of it ought to be the same, the undamaged part, the eternal part.

But the poems and the poetry of the experience both were ephemeral—one written on paper with ink in letters, the other so intangible we can't even talk about it. Better to hold the silence. The silence—held as if physical, but ironically about the absence of the physical body: the folder of poems is gone.

Gray told me, "you have to write to the lost poems now," and so I began writing directly to the condition itself of "lostness." It had something to do with my own silence, even perhaps my shame at keeping silent, at wanting that silence to be beautiful. Silence wrote back as poems.

If it was possible for Silence to write back was it possible—actually possible—for me to speak?

Like many writers I kept a journal by my bedside, either for transcribing dreams roughly in the middle of the night or even for attempting automatic writing while in a half-waking or half-sleeping state, the state when one's inner consciousness is supposedly alert—when one could attempt extreme mental feats like learning a foreign language or memorizing sacred texts simply by hearing them recited. I heard from someone at some point that it was better to allow the dream-worlds to pass unapprehended. Could I damage the pure secrecy of them by trying to write a single version? Wasn't it better then to allow them to pass like a stream, allow those images, phrases, words, and poems, to remain in my subconscious mind to be forever fertile, forever feeding me? Should there be things one *never* says, not even in the darkest places of the night?

I found myself in Cairo summer of 2001 accompanying my father on a business trip. Together we visited the *Ras-ul-Hussain* masjid. A place of secret origins, this masjid was said to be the burial place of the head of Imam Hussain, grandson of the Prophet. Well, mostly Shi'as believe that Hussain—all of him—is actually buried in Karbala, Iraq. Still we found ourselves there, flabbergasted by the intense devotion of the Cairenes—mostly Sunni—to this most Shi'a of saints. My father told us we had to pray there and that if we prayed for anything there it would be granted since it was a place of such intense devotion. What moved him the most were the Sunnis themselves building and preserving this place.

Whether or not anything holy had actually happened there or anything holy was actually buried there was beside the point for him. And for me, it was an actualization of my own sense of spiritual doubt being ultimately the most sacred thing. I found myself in the burial spot where the head of Hussain, severed from his body, was said to be. I knew that if I prayed for something it would become real.

But what could I pray for? To have my body's love and desires disappear, change? To have the courage to speak? When it mattered—when it *really* (strangely) mattered—there was nothing to pray for. Because to "pray" would mean to ask for an answer. I did not want to "receive" an answer, because I wanted my own.

Is prayer panic or in the most perverse way an actual denial of faith? That if God loves you He would come and take away your hardship? And if your hardship is not lessened, what could that mean? How could I pray for something? Was it selfish?

Beyond all that—heartbreakingly—I could not choose what I wanted.

My book of poems *The Far Mosque* was about—in its conceptual form—the changing of the direction of prayer by God from the "far" mosque in Jerusalem to the "near" mosque in Mecca. In the story the Prophet is borne aloft from Mecca to Jerusalem and then up into Heaven to receive instruction. In response to the historical controversy about the actual location of far mosque, Rumi said, "Solomon's mosque is not made of bricks and bars . . . the farthest mosque is the one inside you."

So it might not be so odd that there's always something you are whispering to God that no one else is supposed to hear. The holiest place—the place you can jump up into heaven from—is inside you. There's not such a long way—modern South Asian history notwithstanding, as my wise grandfather instinctively knew—between apparently different religions. In most religions public expression of prayer is preferred and encouraged, but for me poetry and prayer—both ways of talking to God, I guess—depend on secrecy or at least secretiveness. As much as I have ever been public about my life, who I love, how I love him, I had always held it back as a secret from those who knew me the best, the most, the every way.

Whether you are keeping a secret or keeping your silence it comes out in everything you say, every poem you write. I always wanted to tell everything but knew there was a piece of it—not a piece of it, but the thing itself—that I could not tell.

Were the poems I wrote after the loss of the folder practice for a speech I was afraid to give? Is the form of a "prayer" just practice for actually talking to God? After years of comfort with these questions—comfort with silence, comfort with secrecy, comfort with the gifts in poetry they offered me—I found myself at last wanting only to speak.

How I said it I will not yet tell.

After all, every poem has a secret place in it where promises are made.

For so long I worshiped the silence, the quiet place in existence, of being unwilling, or unable, to speak, but more than that, exploring the beauty and mystery of doubt and unknowing.

How much have I been irrevocably changed by this pressure, the way a landscape is sculpted by the glacier as it advances across it, but also as the glacier retreats? Everything feels strange now—my writing in my journal, interacting with friends and colleagues I have known for years, interacting with my partner, Marco. I keep wondering, *can they tell something has happened?* How will poetry and prayer work for me now?

In the *hadith* it is said, "Paradise lies beneath the feet of your mother." It is a part of Islam I find very easy to believe. But the body and the soul might not agree on its meaning. I think there is a place in the "self" where the flesh of the body's temporal existence and the quotidian awareness of the mind and the placid awareness of the eternal (and usually very quiet) soul do not meet. I think that God is the place you cannot go.

For months I wondered to myself, any time I had a moment alone, *When will I be able to go back to my parents' house? When will I hear my mother's voice again? If paradise lies beneath the feet of my mother, how will I get there?*

For a man to leap up into Heaven, he had to go from the near mosque to the far mosque to the "farthest mosque." And what did he hear there? He was sent from silence back to his home—told the direction of worship was what was closest to him. For years I worshiped silence. In a single afternoon, the direction for my prayers changed.

NOTES

1. Jane Cooper, *The Flashboat* (New York: W. W. Norton), 236.

2. Ibid., 58.

3. For more on Revell's complex discussion, see his *Invisible Green: Selected Prose* (Richmond, CA: Omnidawn, 2005).

4. Lisa Mueller, *Second Language* (Baton Rouge: Louisiana State University Press, 1986), 59.

UNDER DISCUSSION
Annie Finch and Marilyn Hacker, General Editors
Donald Hall, Founding Editor

Volumes in the Under Discussion series collect reviews and essays about
individual poets. The series is concerned with contemporary American and
English poets about whom the consensus has not yet been formed and the
final vote has not been taken. Titles in the series include:

On Frank Bidart: Fastening the Voice to the Page
edited by Liam Rector and Tree Swenson
On Louise Glück: Change What You See
edited by Joanne Feit Diehl
On James Tate
edited by Brian Henry
Robert Hayden
edited by Laurence Goldstein and Robert Chrisman
Charles Simic
edited by Bruce Weigl
On Gwendolyn Brooks
edited by Stephen Caldwell Wright
On William Stafford
edited by Tom Andrews
Denise Levertov
edited with an introduction by Albert Gelpi
The Poetry of W. D. Snodgrass
edited by Stephen Haven
On the Poetry of Philip Levine
edited by Christopher Buckley
James Wright
edited by Peter Stitt and Frank Graziano
Anne Sexton
edited by Steven E. Colburn
On the Poetry of Galway Kinnell
edited by Howard Nelson
Robert Creeley's Life and Work
edited by John Wilson
On the Poetry of Allen Ginsberg
edited by Lewis Hyde
Reading Adrienne Rich
edited by Jane Roberta Cooper
Elizabeth Bishop and Her Art
edited by Lloyd Schwartz and Sybil P. Estess